A HISTORY OF IRISH ORGANIZED CRIME

BLOOD, BOMBS, AND TEARS FOR THE HOMELAND

DAVID CARLTON

CONTENTS

INTRODUCTION

Organized crime groups, or what is often colloquially referred to as "the mob," have been a long-held fascination for the public, perhaps made most famous by infamous Italian-American mobsters, such as Al Capone. For many decades, we have morbidly marveled at the antics of the men and women who make crime their lifestyle.

Movies and books have served to glamorize the life of a mobster, ensuring that almost everyone believes that membership in an organized crime syndicate comes with money, flashy cars, great power, and an almost certain violent death before one's time. However, the truth behind these organizations is quite different, as is the reality of the history of organized crime across the world.

When we think about the mob, we likely picture men in suits gathered around tables in Italian restaurants in Brooklyn, N.Y., gambling, smoking, and planning who to take out next. The era we picture is almost always fixed, too—usually the 1920s to the early 1960s. It was during this time that the mainstream press made the most noise about the rampant scourge of organized crime, so you would be forgiven for thinking that this is where and when it started—and ended.

Not only did organized crime have its roots in many countries around the world long before the 1920s, it also, most certainly, was not just an American issue. In fact, some of the most powerful mob families were homegrown in the lush fields of the Emerald Isle of Ireland.

Irish organized crime has played such a major role in the underworld, and even to a certain extent in politics, religion, and society as a whole, that it, without a doubt, warrants its own book. Many different resources have been written and published about the various facets of Ireland's history and politics, but not very many have focused on the common thread that runs through the Emerald Isle, and right across the Atlantic into North America—organized crime.

In this book, I have accumulated my research around a few different areas related to the histories of Ireland, North America, and a few other countries in the world, and the sometimes surprising ways in which those histories run parallel with the establishment and growth of Irish organized crime groups.

Depending on where you find yourself in the world, many of these aspects of history may be new to you. For others, especially if you are of Irish descent, they may be all too familiar. There is one common discovery that all readers will make, regardless of their own geographical background, and that is an understanding of just how deeply entwined the economic, political, and social progress of a country sometimes is with the mob.

In the chapters that follow, we will discover how and why Ireland came to liberate itself from English rule, and what role organized crime may have played in that liberation. If you've ever wondered about the large population of Irish descendants in North America, we'll pull back the curtain on the circumstances that drove hordes of Irish immigrants across the Atlantic, and the difficulties they faced when trying to claim their own American dream.

Although we often think about the politics of a country changing in isolation from the rest of the world, the opposite is more often true. International pressures and alliances often influence what happens within a country's borders, even more so that its own citizens do, and Ireland was no different.

Ireland is often associated with some of the most intense and devastating conflicts in modern history. At the forefront of memories remains clashes between Catholic and Protestant groups, fatal bombings, and the names of groups related to what would forever become known as "The Troubles." As with almost everything in history, though, there are three sides to a story—side A, side B, and the truth. Within the pages of this book, we will draw out surprising and little-known aspects of these seemingly well-known historical events, and how they may well have connections to the underworld.

If you've spent even a short amount of time delving into the history of the Irish mob, or have any Irish family, you've likely heard the names of some of the most notorious Irish mobsters muttered under breath, included in catchy sayings, or uttered as warnings about the evils of the world. Men like Whitey Bulger, James Coonan, and more recently, the Kinahan Gang have long been the stuff of legend, but their stories are often even more fascinating and shocking than history claims. We will delve into some of these well-known names in this book, but we will also look at some of the lesser known characters within the world of Irish organized crime, and the surprising ways in which they often contributed even more to the history books.

To round off our sojourn into the Irish world of organized crime, we'll come full circle and discover the current state of organized crime affairs in Ireland, North America, and across the world, which have evolved in some unexpected ways.

The impact of organized crime has been immense over time, and the truth of it, along with its enormity, we'll attempt to explain in this book.

HISTORY WITH BRITISH RULE

A fossilized reindeer bone discovered in a cave in North Cork recently offered up a different timeline to when human beings can first be historically placed in Ireland. The bone, which was originally unearthed in 1972 (Roseingrave, 2021), was reanalyzed with new technology, and scientists found a chop mark on the bone. This, of course, points to a human having hunted and killed the animal, and it's thanks to that sole reindeer, that we know people were first moving around Ireland up to 33,000 years ago.

Of course, much has happened in 33,000 years, but the most important events, which would contribute to Irish culture and history, included the emergence of Celtic culture around 600 B.C., the emergence of Christianity in the late fourth century A.D., and Viking penetration, which began around 1014, with the Battle of Clontarf.

It would be the Norman invasion in 1169, which would begin more than 800 years of English political and military involvement in Ireland. For the next 300 years, Gaelic resurgence would push back against the Normans, though, until the English had only small pockets of control. Throughout this period, Ireland was a decentralized collection of small territories, and this actually worked in the country's favor. Each separate territory, or túatha, had to be overthrown by the English, in order to exercise any significant extent of control, and this was expensive and time-consuming.

The now infamous ongoing clash between the Protestant and Catholics faiths in Ireland started around 1541, when Henry VIII proclaimed himself King of Ireland, and Protestant Reformation came up against Catholic counter-reformation. Ongoing attempts by England to conquer Norman and Gaelic territories resulted in notable conflicts, such as the first and second Norman rebellions and the Nine Years War (1593—1603). The English brought thousands of Scottish Protestant and English settlers into the country, in the hopes of overwhelming the Hiberno-Norman and Catholic landholders, and Ireland arguably became England's first colony. The Battle of Kinsale, in 1601, resulted in the final defeat of Gaelic Ireland, and the beginning of Ireland's history as part of the English, and at a later stage, the British Empire.

Disputes between the Protestant landholder minority and dispossessed Catholic majority intensified during the 17th century. During this time, and leading up to the 20th century, a political, social, and economic domination of Ireland by Protestants emerged. This is referred to as the Protestant Ascendancy, or more commonly just the Ascendancy. The Ascendancy resulted in other groups, including Roman Catholics, being excluded from politics, and the elite in Ireland during this time were almost entirely made of Protestants. Until the Reform Acts were passed between 1832 and 1928, intense resentment grew among Irish Catholics as they acknowledged that, although they formed the majority, a system was in place that held them entirely under the power of a few.

Catholic landowners were slowly and systematically dispossessed of their land assets. Of course, at this time, land equated directly to power and wealth, so the repercussions of this stretched into the economic and social sphere of the Catholic community. Catholics were not given full rights in the same way Protestants had, until the Catholic Emancipation in 1829.

A natural event in 1845 would have a far-reaching impact both in Ireland and across the ocean in America that changed forever. The Great Famine was a catastrophic event, which resulted in the death of millions of Irish people. It was also the impetus for the immigration of millions of refugees to flee Ireland to America and other countries. We'll talk more about this period in the next chapter, but socially, the Great Famine would become an important turning point in Irish history.

While the Irish fought to simply survive from day to day, English rule strengthened in the country, and the battle for independence was diluted for many decades, overwhelmed by the necessity to simply eat.

However, by the time the British were embroiled right in the thick of the first World War (WWI), which was fought between 1914—1918, an armed insurrection would reignite the fight for independence. The Easter Rising, also known as the Easter Rebellion (1916), was launched by the Irish republicans, in an effort to defeat British rule while that country was so intensely focused on fighting in WWI. It would become the most significant rebellion in 200 years of Irish history, and although its leaders would be executed by British authorities, it would be those very executions that further fired up the desire for independence among the Irish.

From a social, cultural, and political perspective, by the 17th and 18th centuries, Gaelic influences had been all but demolished in the upper echelons of Irish society. However, in small pockets of the people living in lower classes, these ancient traditions and cultures continued, and caused further class-based conflict. Those who continued to practice the so-called pagan traditions of Gaelic culture were seen as unholy and ignorant. The confiscation of land

3

made Ireland a land of great estates, and except for Dublin, small towns began to decay under British trade restrictions.

Culture in the country around this time predominantly followed that of Britain, especially when the numbers of Anglo-Irish increased.

Despite the political and social upheaval in Ireland during this time, the criminal element was already starting to blossom, and one area in particular would become the epicenter of the growth of organized crime within Ireland.

The district, which was at one-time a red-light area in Dublin, was called Monto, and it became infamous for organized criminal activity. The area was contained between Talbot, Amiens, and Gardiner Streets and Seán McDermott Street. The area is called Summerhill today. The name Monto was very simply a shortening of Montgomery Street, which ran parallel to the lower end of Talbot Street, toward Connolly Station. Montgomery Street was named after Elizabeth Montgomery, the wife of the first Viscount Mountjoy, Luke Gardiner.

In Monto's heyday, which stretched roughly between the 1860s and the 1950s, there were believed to be up to 1,600 sex workers working in the area at any given time, with many different classes of customers in which they provided services. During this time, Dublin was believed to have the largest red-light district in the whole of Europe. Profits garnered in this area were improved by the large number of British resident soldiers in the city.

Legend has it that King Edward VII, of England, while still the Prince of Wales, lost his virginity in Monto. In the 1880s, it was reported that the prince, his wife Princess Alexandra, and their son the Duke of Clarence, managed to slip away from their bodyguards, in order to stroll unrecognized through Monto.

In the oral history collection *Dublin Tenement Life*, Kevin Kearns noted that a large majority of the sex wokers in the Monto area were unwed mothers. Societal norms at the time meant that these women would often be disowned by their families and abandoned by the fathers of their babies. While middle class Dubliners viewed these women in a poor light, the devoutly Catholic, but impoverished residents of Monto, called local sex workers "unfortunate girls," and had the understanding that these women had often turned to sex work as a last resort. Kearns relayed that these sex workers were mostly young, attractive women who showed a great sense of kindness toward those less fortunate than them, especially the children who could be found living in the slums.

Perhaps one of the first reported forms of organized crime in this area were the mostly female owners of brothels, or *kips*. The women who ran the brothels, also referred to as madams, would go on to become some of the greatest legends in Dublin folklore. These were mostly women who had been born and bred in Dublin. These women were tough and shrewd businesswomen and they ruled their businesses in a strict, but maternal manner. The young women who worked as sex workers in these brothels often ended up there as the lesser of two evils. They could either go to convents, where their illegitimate babies would be taken away from them, and would essentially be indentured servants to the nuns. Or they could go to the brothels, where the madams clothed them and housed them. In return, the madams also took a large cut of their earnings. Many of the brothels also illegally sold alcohol, which certainly helped to encourage clients to part with their money. Many of the madams grew a large amount of wealth. They wore expensive jewels, drove cars—which at the time was a mark of wealth—and their children attended expensive schools overseas. Some of the madams were very controlling of their workers and kept them detained in the brothels. This is where the concept of human trafficking—which would become a huge part of the organized crime repertoire—began. For the most part in Monto, sex workers were in the brothels of their own choice, but considering that choice was one of two very poor options, we must wonder how much true consent was really involved in that situation.

The concept of street gangs, perhaps one of the most basic forms of organized crime, also began in Monto. Four gangs were most prominent in the area at the time: the Stafford street gang, the Ash street gang, the Sheriff street gang, and the Monto gang. The members of these gangs were predominantly men who worked in the coal industry—strapping, tough men who could consume alcohol in vast quantities. For the most part, these gangs brawled against each other for dominance in the area. These brawls were not just fist fights. Very early on, weapons were involved, including knives, brass knuckles, and iron bars.

It was also around this time in Monto that the line between organized crime and the wealthiest and most prominent of citizens started to become blurred. The brothels were often patronized by men who held a high level of standing in society—soldiers, generals, businessmen, and sometimes even members of the clergy.

So Monto was most certainly a geographical starting point for organized crime in Ireland. It is a physical place that we can point to, in which some of the most interesting and, at times, frightening organized crime activity had its roots. However, the overlap between organized crime, Irish politics, and the fight for independence is also starkly evident in Monto. This is an aspect we'll discuss further later on in this book, but we cannot avoid the knowledge, even at this point, that as street gangs were developing, and brothels were growing, simultaneously groups like the Irish Republican Army (IRA) were also putting down roots in Monto. The links were inextricably formed.

2

THE AMERICAN DREAM

Although the 19th century is often credited as the period in which the most Irish immigrants found their way to America, there were actually two separate periods of movement.

During colonial times, many Irish people were already moving to America. These immigrants were predominantly Catholic, and sought to escape the inequity of Protestant Ascendancy. The more Protestants who took control of Ireland and pushed Catholics down, refusing them the right to own land, vote, and succeed in any way, the more these people fled to the land over the ocean. Proof of this early Irish immigrant wave can be found in the Declaration of Independence (1776), which was signed by Charles Carroll. Carroll's signature belonged to the grandson of the original Charles Carroll, who immigrated to America from Ireland in 1706 (Library of Congress, n.d.).

It would, however, be the 19th century that would bring a huge wave of Irish immigrants to America's shores, and also spark the beginning of Irish organized crime in the U.S. In 1845, a fungus called Potato Blight decimated Ireland's potato crops. The blight had started in Europe, and soon spread to Ireland. What made this such a devastating event was that the potato was a staple food in Ireland, and the variety grown there was most susceptible to the fungus, meaning almost every crop throughout the country was completely inedible. Unfortunately, the fungus also damaged the soil that the potatoes were grown in, which meant that there was no hope of future crops for some time. This decimation of the Irish staple food sparked what is now known as the Great Irish Famine. The Gaelic phrase referred to this time was "An Drochshaol," which translates to "Bad Times." This phrase perhaps better portrays how devastating it was to the Irish people. Within five years, this would result in the deaths of at least one million Irish people. At the same time, almost half a million Irish people arrived in America.

Census figures in Ireland clearly show the dramatic decline in population figures throughout the 19th century. In 1841, a census put the population of Ireland at 8.2 million. A decade later, it had declined to 6.6 million, and by 1891, it had almost halved from the 1841 number at 4.7 million. Between 1820 and 1930, it is estimated that as many as 4.5 million Irish arrived in America (Library of Congress, n.d.).

In the 1840s, nearly half of all immigrants who arrived in the U.S. were Irish. Before the famine, almost all Irish immigrants to America were males, while during and post-famine, immigrants were comprised of entire families. This indicates that before the famine happened, opportunities in Ireland were already few and far between, especially for Catholic people, and men would likely have been emigrating to the United States in the hopes of earning money that perhaps they would one day bring home, when things changed in their home country. However, when the famine hit, and for many years afterwards, emigrating was a matter of survival for many Irish people.

During this time, most Irish immigrants were coming from a rural lifestyle, where there was very little modern industry and, as such, their arrival in America came as a culture shock. The people immigrating to America at this time were not necessarily the poorest of their ilk, as the most destitute in Irish would not even have been able to come up with the cost of passage. However, they were still people not used to the industrialized, urban centers they found themselves in once they arrived in the U.S.

Many had spent their entire life savings on the fare to cross, and as such, were unable to move anywhere else in America, so they would settle in the port in which they disembarked. In time, the number of Irish people in New York City would exceed the number in Dublin, Ireland.

Irish immigrants during this time would implement patterns of choices that immigrants would follow for decades to come. This included their housing choices, how they sent financial support to families back in Ireland, the occupations they entered into, and even how their choice to emigrate influenced their extended families back in Ireland to make the move. Irish immigrants were mostly forced to live in crowded subdivisions that were built for single families. Any empty space, such as attics and cellars, became make-do homes for desperate immigrants. These close quarters, as well as the fact that sewage and running water quickly became wholly inadequate, meant that disease spread quickly among immigrants. Cholera, typhus, and tuberculosis moved rapidly through the Irish-American population, but the miserable living conditions, and the hostility these people faced from some Americans resulted in severe depression, and other mental health issues.

Although opportunities for work in America certainly exceeded those in Ireland, most immigrants would have to be happy with entering the workforce at the bottom of the ladder, and often doing the menial jobs that most Americans did not want to do.

As Irish immigrants began to move inland, and competition for jobs with Americans-by-birth increased, they found themselves the target of hatred, and groups such as the American Protective Association (APA) and the Ku Klux Klan (KKK) also antagonized them. Over time, Irish-Americans would start to climb the occupational, social, and economic ladder, and second and third generation Irish-Americans were, on average, far more successful than their original immigrant parents.

If Irish immigrants thought that by leaving Ireland they would also leave behind the religious conflict between Protestants and Catholics, they would be disappointed. Verbal attacks between groups often escalated to mob violence, as well as destruction of property. One particularly deadly incident occurred in 1831, in New York City, when a Protestant group burned down St. Mary's Catholic Church; and in 1844, religious conflict escalated into a riot in Philadelphia, where 13 people died.

THE RISE OF GANGS ACROSS AMERICA

The street gang concept soon spread with the Irish from Monto in their homeland, to their new home. Such gangs became prolific, at first, in many of the port cities the immigrants inhabited, and later inland, too.

New York City was one of the most popular cities where Irish immigrants saw some of the first of these gangs. The Dead Rabbits was run by an Irish immigrant named John Morrissey, who would later go on to become a congressman. Along with another New York gang, the Whyos, the Dead Rabbits dominated New York's underworld for close to a century. However, in the 1890s, these two gangs began to face competition from gangs made up of other immigrant groups, including Italians. In the early 1900s, though, Irish-American gangs were once again ruling the Big Apple, with the Five Points Gang, the Hudson Dusters, and the Gopher Gang, among others, emerging as strong players. In New York, at least, likely because it was a port town for many immigrant groups, the pendulum of power would frequently swing between the Italian and the Irish gangs.

When Italian gangs like the Morello crime family began to appear, a decision was made to unite many of the existing Irish gangs into one formidable force—the White Hand Gang. Although this unified gang was initially successful at keeping the Italian crime families at bay in New York, the various factions within the White Hand Gang began to fight against one another, and this, combined with the unstable leadership, led to its downfall by 1925. The New York waterfront would, at this point, fall back under the control of Italian mobsters for some time.

We'll chat more about another group, the Westies, later on in this book, as their contribution to Irish organized crime was significant enough to warrant a deeper look, but it's worth noting here that the gang found its roots in Hell's Kitchen.

The Roach Guards were a criminal gang that operated in New York in the early 19th century. The gang was originally developed as a protection crew, but soon started committing robbery and murder. Also in New York, around this same time, was the Patsy Conroy Gang, which was a group of river pirates active on the waterfront in New York City after the American Civil War, which was fought between 1861—1865 (Wikipedia Contributor, 2022).

Another interesting New York gang was the Boodle Gang, which was active in the mid to late 19th century as butcher cart thieves. During this time, the price of meat was exorbitant, so it was a valuable item, and the Boodle Gang figured out they could capitalize on this by hijacking butchers as they transported their products, and then sell the meat on what was referred to as the black market. A black market is the term given to the illegal trade of scarce or illicit commodities.

Boston would become a significant hotspot for Irish-American organized crime, particularly in areas with high Irish immigrant numbers, such as Charlestown, Somerville, South Boston,

Roxbury, and Dorchester. Boston saw Irish gangsters rising up, for the most part, during Prohibition—the nationwide ban on the production, distribution, sale, and consumption of alcohol between 1920 and 1933. Boston's underworld was dominated by the Gustin Gang, headed by Frank Wallace, until he died in 1931, at the hands of Italian gangsters. Another infamous Irish-American gang would have its start in Boston—the Winter Hill Gang. We'll get into this gang more in a later chapter, as they played a large role in the Irish-American organized crime scene.

Philadelphia had its own Irish gangs, even pre-Prohibition. The Schuylkill Rangers were headed up by Jimmy Haggerty. Haggerty would prove his power in Philadelphia, after evading the long hand of the law on many occasions. This shows that, even this early on, corrupt law enforcement was already closely entwined in organized crime. Haggerty was arrested only once, in 1865, but eight months later, he received a full pardon from Gov. Andrew Curtin. However, Haggerty would push the line too far in 1869, when he shot and wounded a police officer, and then, it would seem that all of his connections would not be enough to get him out of that situation. Haggerty fled, though, and eventually, the wounded officer was paid hush money to keep things to himself, and Haggerty was once again free as a bird.

After World War II (WWII), which was fought between 1939—1945, the K&A Gang would become the dominant Irish gang in Philadelphia. The gang was a multi-generational, highly-organized group of Irish immigrants and Irish-Americans. K&A started out as a youth street gang, which grew more and more powerful, as locals and blue-collar workers decided to join, in the hopes of earning extra income. Over time, K&A expanded, became even more organized, and established themselves in lucrative crime markets, such as loan-sharking, gambling, and burglary. The K&A Gang was one that would outlast most Philly gangs, joining the methamphetamine trade in the 1980s. In 1987, several members of the

K&A Gang would be indicted for their involvement in drug trafficking.

Chicago was another hotspot for Irish-American organized crime and gangs. Michael McDonald had set up his criminal empire pre-Prohibition, and his successors would take over during Prohibition, and move into hijacking and bootlegging activities. However, it would not be long, until some infamous Italian mobsters, including Al Capone, would begin to rival the Irish in the Windy City.

During this time, in Cleveland, the so-called Irishtown Bend, Ohio City, Whiskey Island, Detroit Shoreway, and Haymarket neighborhoods—predominantly inhabited by Irish-Americans—became breeding grounds for gangs. The McCart Street Gang, the Cheyenne Gang, and the Blinky Morgan Gang all became notorious in the area. The latter gang became very well-known after one robbery they were involved in, in which a detective was killed. This was an interesting case study in law enforcement's attempts to curb organized crime, because a reward was offered in this case, and undercover officers were even sent to infiltrate the gang, which resulted in all its members being apprehended.

Irish immigrants were known for being excellent at boxing, and it would be this sport that would often become inextricably linked with organized crime throughout history. This started in Cleveland when Thomas McGinty, a former professional featherweight boxer, became one of the city's biggest bootleggers, who also expanded into illegal gambling. McGinty was a member of the Cleveland Syndicate, which was a mish-mash of Irish-Americans, Jewish Americans, and Italians. The syndicate was split into factions, however, along those lines. The syndicate's main activity was gambling and they spread out into Las Vegas, and even Cuba, with their casinos and horse racing setups.

After WWII, the Kilbane brothers were prominent on the Cleveland organized crime scene, and had their feelers in prostitution, loan-sharking, and gambling rackets. It would also emerge that they had been running murder-for-hire jobs, and it would be this crime that would be the Kilbane brothers' eventual downfall, when they were found guilty of having carried out two murders-for-hire.

An interesting new branch in the organized crime world would first be seen in Detroit, when the Joseph 'Legs' Laman Gang began to specialize in what would be known as the "snatch racket." This involved kidnapping wealthy gamblers and bootleggers, and holding them for ransom. This type of crime would become a very popular form of organized crime in later years, especially in South American countries. At the time, many of the snatching crimes in Detroit were incorrectly attributed to another gang, called the Purple Gang, but it would eventually emerge they were mostly the work of the Laman Gang. The kidnapping of those involved in the underworld worked well for the gang, because the victims would usually not go to police, due to their own criminal connections. The Laman Gang's downfall in this respect came when they started to kidnap legitimate businessmen, whose families did not think twice about involving law enforcement.

In New Orleans, the Terminal Gang was made up of several members of the Irish Channel neighborhood. The political connection to organized crime was once again highlighted here, when the Terminal Gang was found to have connections to the Democratic Mayor Martin Behrem. The Terminal Gang was named for the Terminal station where many of the members also worked as drivers. The gang would engage in gambling, narcotics, and illegal alcohol rings. They also used their roles as drivers to rob fares. The gang eventually collapsed after Mayor Behrem lost his seat in office.

In Oklahoma City, where the Aryan Brotherhood already had its roots very early on, an Irish prison gang emerged, which styled itself as an alternative to this white supremacist group. They expanded from dealing drugs in prison to trafficking of drugs in Kansas, California, and Oklahoma.

In Toledo, Ohio, an Irish immigrant named Jack Kennedy controlled nightclubs and bootlegging. He became involved in a turf war with Thomas Licavoli's Gang. An enforcer from the Licavoli Gang ended up killing Kennedy and three other nightclub owners. This was one of the first instances in which Irish organized crime had been involved in the nightclub industry, and showed how its reach had stretched.

With Irish-American organized crime on the rise in American cities, it would soon branch out into other countries, too, and many of the links formed during this time would last well into the next few decades.

3

THE IRISH MAKE GLOBAL NEWS

When Irish immigrants arrived in America, they not only put down roots in society, the economy, and in the religious community, some also brought with them the street gang concept. Many of these street gangs evolved into sophisticated criminal organizations, and the reach of Irish organized crime soon became global.

Other countries in which Irish organized crime became popular included Canada, Spain, England, and Australia.

The West End Gang is one of Canada's most powerful criminal organizations. It began in the early 1900s, and is still in existence today. Based predominantly in Montreal, the West End Gang did not become particularly powerful until around the 1960s. Before that, they were known very simply as the "Irish Gang." In the early days, the West End Gang focused on home invasions, truck hijackings, protection rackets, kidnapping, extortion, armed robbery, and drug trafficking.

In the 1970s, the West End Gang moved almost exclusively into drug trafficking. They started importing cocaine and hashish during this time, and by using their Irish gang contacts in America, as well as other contacts in Europe and South America, they became one of the biggest drug dealing organizations in America and Canada. Many of the West End Gang members worked out of Florida. Since the 1970s, the West End Gang has formed connections with the Cosa Nostra, the Hells Angels, the Montreal Mafia, and some Colombian cartels.

Spain may seem a strange location for Irish organized crime to extend into, but it is a very popular holiday destination for British tourists, and as a result, the Kinahan Cartel decided to establish a stronghold in this country in 2003. They chose Costa del Sol as their base of operations, and set up drug trafficking and money laundering rackets in the country. Led by Christy and Daniel Kinahan, the cartel amassed a huge number of exotic vehicles, firearms, and properties. However, the Kinahan hold on Spain would not be without its difficulties, and in May 2010, Spanish and Irish police conducted a joint operation called Operation Shovel, which led to the arrest of 22 members of the Kinahan Cartel. However, the members were soon released without charge, due to lack of evidence.

The organized crime link to Spain goes further back than this though. In 1978, a 100-year-old extradition treaty between Spain and the United Kingdom expired. The treaty was replaced in 1985, and by that time, the Costa del Sol on Spain's southern coast was filled with British and Irish fugitives and criminals. This influx gave rise to the term "Costa del Crime."

Although many Irish immigrants headed to America during and after the Great Famine, some ran out of money and ended up staying in port towns like Liverpool, England. This made many of these port towns havens for Irish immigrants, in much the same way that American port towns were, and a similar rise in Irish organized crime began there, too.

In addition, just as Irish-Americans had continued to face religious intolerance in their new country, those left behind in

England found themselves in the same position, except, for them, the situation was worse. Irish Catholics in England were not just persecuted for their religion, they were also persecuted because they were Irish. The historical issues between Ireland and England also meant that confrontations between gangs formed by people of Irish descent and English gangs were even more violent.

For the Irish in England, forming gangs became very much about self protection, and the criminal element only came much later. This anti-Irish sentiment would go on in England for many years to come and, as a result, young boys who grew up feeling persecuted simply because of their country of origin, often became some of the most violent organized criminals in British history. Violence and self-protection had simply been the staple food of their youths, and they knew nothing else.

Irish author and ex-criminal Noel 'Razor' Smith, grew up in England under these conditions and he recalled the feeling that, among the poor Irish community in England, being a criminal was very normal. For children, especially boys in these families, there were no dreams of what they would become when they were older —they all knew they would become involved in a criminal enterprise of some form or another. When Smith was in prison, he recalled that many of the prisoners were of Irish descent. He said that, for as long as he has remembered, the feeling among his kinspeople was one of needing to fight back against the system. For most, this resulted in them becoming militarized and committing crimes to lash out. In English prisons, most of the wardens were English ex-army, and this only added to the conflict behind bars.

One of the most notorious and violent Irish criminal organizations in England was the Bradish Brothers Gang. They ran a gang of armed robbers in the late 1990s and early 2000s. They are believed to have carried out as many as 200 robberies. The Bradish brothers' parents moved to England from their birthplace of Limerick, Ireland. They learned their trade while running with the Dirty Dozen Gang, which was another Irish-led gang in England.

As previously mentioned, the sport of boxing was often linked with organized crime and there was a time when Irish-born Gaelic football players living in England were also well known for their criminal antics. Jimmy "The Danger" Beirne was a player of the Roscommon Gaelic football team that famously defeated Kildare, in the 1966 All-Ireland final. When he moved to London in the late 70s, he started trading in gold Krugerrands. Krugerrands are gold coins that were minted in the Republic of South Africa in 1960s to help promote South African gold in international markets and so individuals could own gold. Krugerrands are among the most regularly traded gold coins in the world market. After serving some time in prison, he briefly returned to Ireland, but was soon back in London, this time participating in the drug trade.

However, there are also some sporting turnaround stories in the Irish criminal underworld, such as Ray Bishop, who was once Britain's most wanted man. Bishop was a drug smuggler, armed robber, and human trafficker. He developed an addiction to heroin and cocaine. After being imprisoned for one of his many crimes, though, Bishop made a remarkable turnaround. He got clean, took up boxing, and went on to become British Middleweight Boxing Champion.

Australia, like Spain, is another country in which one would not necessarily expect to find connections to Irish organized crime, but they are there all the same. One Australian man with very strong connections to Irish organized crime was the late Murray Riley. This former policeman, turned international drug trafficker, became involved with the Provisional Irish Republican Army (Provos), when he found himself on the run in Ireland and needed assistance in order to remain in hiding. During this time, he developed relationships with the leaders of the Provos and, when he returned to Australia, started to smuggle heroin between

Ireland and Australia, with assistance from the Provos. Riley was also connected with Irish-American gangsters and he helped many of them to flee to Australia and start new lives (McDowell, 2021).

However, Australian connections to Irish organized crime started long before Riley. In the late 1800s, Edward Ned Kelly, a son of Irish parents, was an outlaw and gang leader in Australia. Kelly and his gang members were notorious robbers, and they pulled off many heists across Victoria. Kelly himself was also known as a murderer of multiple policemen, and this put him on the most wanted list in Australia for many years. He was eventually captured, convicted, and executed for his crimes in 1880, when he was just 25 years old.

The reach of Irish organized crime internationally is well established, but it had another consequence. Although these immigrants had left their home country, they had not given up on hopes of independence for their motherland, and their presence and power in the international community soon encouraged the world to get behind Ireland's fight.

As WWI came to an end, the nations that had emerged notorious gathered their leadership officers in 1919, in France, allegedly to restructure the world so there would never be a need for another world war. In reality, what these nations were doing was restructuring borders so their nations would be as large as possible. The end of the war had presented several opportunities for this, including splitting up the remains of the Ottoman Empire. In a territory of one of the victors—England—the seeds of discontent had long been sewn. The way in which the events taking place in Ireland would be reported by the international press, and would have serious ramifications for the Irish fight for independence.

What follows is an account of the general road to Irish independence. Although we will provide a deeper look into the individual organizations and parties in later chapters, it is important for us, at this point, to have a general overview of events and players that contributed to independence.

On Jan. 21, 1919, several recently elected Irish Sinn Féin MPs got together and formed their own parliament. Sinn Féin is an Irish republican and democratic socialist political party active throughout both the Republic of Ireland and Northern Ireland.

They also affirmed a declaration for an independent Irish Republic, which had been proclaimed, in 1916 on Easter Sunday. On Jan. 25, 1919, the group sent a delegation to the aforementioned Peace Conference in Paris, which was completely ignored (Gannon, n.d.). Also on this same day, Sinn Féin volunteers attacked and killed two policemen in Tipperary, Ireland. This event would mark the beginning of a violent guerrilla war, commonly referred to as the Irish War of Independence, that seemed to gain intensity with every month that passed.

The Restoration of Order in Ireland Act (ROIA), which was passed in August 1920, allowed for continued strict control over Irish press. At the time, *The Irish Times* newspaper represented the Irish Unionist viewpoint. The paper generally reported the official version of whichever story was news at the time. Other large newspapers in Ireland had to tread a fine line between official repression and reporting the truth. These other newspapers often condemned IRA violence, reported relatively fairly on Sinn Féin activities, and often revealed the violence of English forces. In 1920, the owners and editor of the *Freeman's Journal* were handed down one year's imprisonment, through the conditions of the ROIA.

The media office for Dublin Castle was directed by army captains who kept a sharp eye on the outflow of information. As a result, it produced news that was heavily laden with blatant propaganda. The propaganda usually took the form of English forces having the "murder-machine" at their mercy, and that the English were always on the verge of domination. The castle issued an official summary each week, which usually contained many half-truths and blatant lies.

On the other end of the spectrum, the *Irish Bulletin*, which was a news sheet produced by the Dáil Propaganda Department, gained a reputation for reporting accurately. The Bulletin was circulated internationally, and it essentially presented the republican view. For reporters on the continent, the *Bulletin* provided an alternative source of information to the publications that were Dublin Castle-fed. This also helped to spread an alternative message in North America, Europe, South Africa, and Australia.

In 1920, as reprisals and fatalities increased, international interest in Ireland increased and many American, British, and journalists from around the continent arrived in Dublin to get a first-hand view. A few of these journalists contacted Sinn Féin. The group treated the journalists with courtesy. Of course, there was also the hope that some may gain access to secret interviews with some of the leading republican figures to add to the journalistic interest. At first, a large majority of the press in Britain reported the official version, without much interpretation. In those stories, events were cast as a war between police and Sinn Féin's "murderous criminal conspiracy."

Certain newspapers, such as the *Morning Post*, often mindlessly repeated the official propaganda that was produced throughout the conflict. Other publications, such as the *Daily News* and *Manchester Guardian*, preferred an independent slant, and would become more critical of government policy as it related to Irish matters, as time progressed. Many publications presented the violence carried out by the IRA as criminal, however, in time, they would come to see it as a result of repression and poor governance.

By 1921, a sense of unease was increasing in Britain. In those days, the British Empire was represented in the public domain as existing on a platform of equity, freedom, and justice. The reality of the news coming out of Ireland was in direct contrast to public opinion, and it began to cut away the whole impression the world had of the empire. Sir Hamar Greenwood, British Chief Secretary for Ireland, refused to provide any real updates in Parliament and denied some of the press accounts of atrocities occurring in Ireland. However, a cabinet member said that the controversial reporting was "upsetting to their nerves."

One specific feature of the reporting happening on the continent, especially Italy and France, was the mass of weekly print sheets in which important events were portrayed by means of illustrations. From 1919—21, these print sheets would start to report, in dramatic fashion, some of the most important incidents that occurred during the Irish War of Independence. This reporting was not necessarily accurate, because for the most part, the British press agencies' telling of events would be accepted. This narrative often only provided the Dublin Castle point of view.

However, some exceptions to this behavior did occur. In the September 1920 edition of *Le Petit Journal of Paris*, for instance, a printed illustration showed the lord mayor of Cork, Terence MacSwiney, during his hunger-strike. The illustration also showed a Capuchin priest ministering to him, and the caption read, "Le Martyr Irlandais," which translates to "The Irish Martyr." Capuchin priests are members of the Order of Friars Minor Capuchin (O.F.M.Cap.) The priests in this order live austere lives as virtual hermits (Petruzzello, n.d.). There would be a huge outpouring of international sympathy for MacSwiney's hunger strike and resulting death. The event and coverage even caused Benito Mussolini, who was at the time the editor of the Fascist newspaper, *Il Popullo d'Italia*, to report with a sympathetic tone on MacSwiney's death. Strong support was shown to Sinn Féin, and Ireland's struggle for independence was linked to Italy's own similar struggle.

Unofficial uprisings, as well as the burning of Irish towns by English forces, increased in frequency and intensity during the latter half of 1920. An event referred to as "The Sack of Balbriggan," occurred on Sept. 20, 1920, which gained a huge amount of notoriety. The event happened near Dublin, providing easy access for journalists. Many houses were burnt, and a large portion of the population had to evacuate the town. The horrifying images and accompanying copy quickly spread around the world. *La Tribuna Illustrata* printed illustrations of women abandoning the ruins of the town, with the caption translated as, "The Terror in Ireland."

Reprisals within Ireland continued, despite this reporting, and took a more official slant when, in 1921, martial law was introduced in Munster. However, even worse news awaited the British in late 1920, when the first Bloody Sunday took place, followed by the Kilmichael ambush, in which 17 Elite Auxiliaries lost their lives to the IRA.

The British were especially concerned about the opinions of the United States. Although Britain had previously been the dominant world power, this was in fast and noticeable decline, and Britain felt vulnerable to America and its increasing authority. Britain saw the U.S. as being vulnerable to influence by the millions of Irish-Americans in their population. However, in reality, President Warren Harding had shown no interest in Ireland.

Some American journalists were particularly interested in what was happening in Ireland. Most notably, *New Republic* reporter Francis Hackett, and *Philadelphia Public Ledger* reporter Carl Ackermann, both reported the Irish conflict in depth and with clear insight. The rest of the press in the United States took a more neutral stance. When the *New York Times* reported on the burning of Cork on Dec. 13, 1920, they relayed that there had been a 15 million dollar loss in property; it also reported that large numbers of British Auxiliaries were marching through the streets and stopping pedestrians, after their colleagues were ambushed. However, the general tone of the reporting was that the fire had been a random event and no clear blame was laid at any door.

For the most part, American newspapers used feeds from the press agencies without questioning, but the true reality of the British forces' wrongdoings still managed to find its way through. Another blow to the reputation of the British was struck by an organization called the American Commission on Conditions in Ireland, which released some shocking conclusions in 1921. These findings included a determination that the Irish people were at the mercy of British forces in conditions referred to as 'terrorism.' Around this time, British Prime Minister Winston Churchill sent instructions to his cabinet to offer some respite to the people of Ireland. This was mainly because the news from there was becoming damaging to Britain's reputation and relationships with other countries.

By the middle of 1921, as the IRA was mounting increasingly organized ambushes on British forces, authorities in Britain moved between an intensification of their push against the War of Independence, and the possibility of negotiating peace. Generals in the British army situated in Ireland were continuing to insist that they only needed another four months to deliver victory.

The liberal peace camp was unhappy about the atrocities being undertaken by the British in Ireland and the conflict of opinion it caused both nationally and internationally. The British continued to shift between starting peace talks, or flooding Ireland with soldiers to completely overwhelm any resistance. They would eventually opt to start negotiations.

Negotiations would lead to what is now known as the Treaty of December 1921, which resulted in a form of limited independence for 26 Irish counties. Unfortunately, the complete dismissal of the request for an entirely independent republic to be formed would be the cause of a civil war, which broke out within six months (Barry, 2020).

The American press' tendency to report on stories from a terrorism angle is infamous. It's almost expected, in fact, but for some reason, in the Irish conflict, this was different. It may well be because the U.S. has such a huge number of residents of Irish descent, and as such, journalists were given a different perspective on this particular issue. Or perhaps the media simply saw something in Ireland's struggle that resonated with Americans. Either way, on most occasions, when the IRA has engaged in conflict in Ireland, the American press has not condemned their actions in the way one would expect.

It is important to remember, however, that one of the IRA's most significant sources of support is based in New York. In 1981, the Irish Northern Aid Committee (NORAID) was convicted by a U.S. District Court of violating the Foreign Agents Registration Act of 1938, as they had failed to list the IRA as its principal foreign agent (Jones, 1987).

In their fundraising letters in 1971 and 1972, NORAID states that their support is provided exclusively to the Provisional IRA and their affiliates. According to these letters, the funds from NORAID were channeled through Joe Cahill, of Belfast, Ireland, and were used for the advancement of the campaign in Northern Ireland. However, NORAID's publicity director claimed that they did not simply send money and guns to the IRA. Instead, he said they helped to support the families of Irish political prisoners. We'll discuss NORAID in more detail in the next chapter, but suffice to say, the fight for independence in Ireland has always been an international effort, and there has always been a very fine line between organized crime and the support for this fight.

This American view on terrorism would play an interesting, if ironic, role in the Irish fight for independence when on Sept. 11, 2001, the U.S. became the site of the most deadly terrorist attack in recorded history. The *Belfast Telegraph* reported on the link between these two seemingly unconnected events. The article, published Sept. 6, 2011, was written by a journalist of Irish descent, who lived in the Riverdale area of the Bronx, N.Y.

Riverdale is an area filled with second and third generation Irish-Americans. Although many of the Irish-Americans living in Riverdale had long left their poverty-ridden pasts behind them, they had brought along their politics. This was clearly evident in Riverdale, where bars would host pro-IRA events and some of NORAID's most active participants lived in the area. The journalist in question had lived most of his life in Belfast, and when he moved to his wife's family home in Riverdale, he would have been forgiven for thinking that he'd left any terrorism behind. Unfortunately, within days of arriving in Riverdale, al-Qaeda flew several passenger jets into buildings in New York. Al-Qaeda, is a broad-based militant Islamist organization which was founded in the late 1980s by Osama bin Laden. It operates mostly within Afghanistan and surrounding countries. It would be this act of terrorrism by the group, the journalist said, that would not only deeply change America, but also significantly impact Irish politics.

The first sign of this came in Riverdale itself when, a day after the attacks, residents all raised American flags in front of their homes, and they mostly stayed there for the next decade. It was reminiscent of actions taken by Irish citizens during significant events, such as the Shankill Road event or the Falls. The Shankill Road bombing was carried out on Oct. 23, 1993, by the Provos, and became one of the most well-known incidents of the Troubles in Northern Ireland. The Falls were infamous riots which occurred in August 1969, in which six Catholics were killed and several streets were burnt out near Falls Road.

When the American president at the time, George W. Bush spoke the iconic words, "You're either with us, or you're with the terrorists," this hit home for Irish-Americans. After all, the organization they supported and pinned their hopes on to free their homeland, the IRA, had been called a terrorist organization on more than one occasion. And while the situation in America seemed clearly different from what was happening in Ireland, it struck a chord. By this time, the IRA had begun peace negotiations, but they still refused to give up their weapons. Many Irish-Americans started to ask why the IRA would refuse to give up its weapons, unless they, too, were planning on carrying out an attack on the scale of 9/11? To the IRA, the most significant home for the operations outside of Ireland was suddenly not the sure thing it had always been.

The American ambassador to the Irish peace process, Richard Haass, was in Ireland on 9/11. He was there to investigate allegations that the IRA had been training American enemy forces in Colombia, but when the planes hit, his message changed. He immediately told the IRA and Sinn Féin representatives that the only way they could redeem themselves was by handing over their weapons.

Quite ironically, though, this major world force giving them an ultimatum may have been just what the IRA and Sinn Féin leaders actually wanted. In reality, for a long time, the hardline stance on not handing over their weapons had been purely for their supporters' benefit. They knew that this was what their supporters wanted to hear, even though the leadership knew it to be an unsustainable position. While they had to continually reassure their followers that the fight would never be given up, they also simultaneously understood that they would have no place in an independent parliament while they still held arms. They also knew that the peace brokering process was not going anywhere any time soon, as long as they continued to hold arms. Therefore, in a way, 9/11 gave them the out they needed.

Six weeks after the planes hit the buildings in America and thousands of people lost their lives, the IRA began to destroy their weaponry. There was little protest from their followers, who understood that the global sentiment had instantly shifted.

There were other actions that emanated in Arab countries, which would impact the Irish situation as well. Colonel Gaddafi, who was deposed as Libya's leader, was often targeted for supporting the IRA, but his doing so actually helped to make the peace process possible. In 1987, the capture of the gun-running ship, Eksund, cut off the IRA's last chance at military success, and shipments of weapons received from the Libyan leader gave the IRA valuable bargaining material, which helped to make the peace process more inviting for the British.

4

THE ORGANIZATIONS

As we've alluded to in previous chapters, there were several Irish organizations that took part in the struggle for independence. Many of these can be inextricably linked to organized crime in Ireland, often through necessity.

In this chapter, we delve into the roles these organizations played, where they came from, what they stood for, and how each may have contributed to the general Irish fight for independence, as well as their links to organized crime.

Irish Republican Army (IRA), which was also called the Provisional Irish Republican Army, was a republican paramilitary organization that sought to establish a republic, end British rule in Northern Ireland, and reunify Ireland.

The IRA was established in 1919. It served as a successor organization to the Irish Volunteers, which was a militant nationalist organization that was founded in 1913. The purpose of the IRA was to render British rule in Ireland inept, through the use of armed force. This would serve its broader objective of forming an independent republic. This objective was pursued by Sinn Féin at a political level. Sinn Féin was the Irish nationalist party.

From the point of its inception, though, the IRA ensured that it operated independently of any political control. During some periods in Irish history, it actually took a dominant role in the independence movement. Many members of the IRA were also members of Sinn Féin.

During the Irish War of Independence (Anglo-Irish War), between 1919—21, the IRA, which was under leadership of Michael Collins, used guerrilla tactics such as raids, ambushes, and sabotage to give the British government no other choice than to negotiate (Arthur & Cowell-Meyers, 2019). As a result, it was decided that two new political entities would be formed: the Irish Free State and Northern Ireland. The Irish Free State was made up of 26 counties and was given dominion status inside the British Empire. Northern Ireland comprised six counties and was occasionally referred to as the province of Ulster, and still a part of the United Kingdom. These terms were not acceptable to a large number of the IRA's members. As a result, the organization split into two factions. The first faction remained under Michael Collins's leadership and supported the treaty. The second faction was under the leadership of Eamon de Valera and opposed the treaty. Michael Collins's group would become the core of the official Irish Free State Army, and Eamon de Valera's group, who were known as 'Irregulars,' started to organize armed resistance against the new government.

The Irish Civil War which ensued, lasted from 1922—23, and came to an end when the Irregulars surrendered. However, they did not surrender their arms or disband. De Valera would go on to lead some members of the Irregulars into parliamentary politics, when Fianna Fáil was created in the Irish Free State. Fianna Fáil is the republican party in Ireland. It is largely a conservative and Christian-democratic political party. Some Irregulars members would remain in the background, though, as an ongoing reminder to future governments that the desire for reunification was still alive, and it would be achieved by force, if need be.

Illegal drilling and recruiting by the IRA continued, accompanied by occasional acts of violence. The IRA was declared illegal in 1931, and once again in 1936. In 1939, after a string of bombings in England by the IRA, stringent measures were taken against the group. This included provisions for internment without trial. Essentially, the government gave themselves the ability to hold political prisoners of war without officially being at war. The British were significantly embarrassed by the IRA's activities during WWII. At one point, the IRA even sought assistance from German Nazi leader Adolf Hitler, in order to help get the British out of Ireland. During this time, five IRA leaders were put to death, and many more were incarcerated without trial.

In 1949, when Ireland withdrew from the British Commonwealth, the IRA started to press for the unification of the Irish republic, which was mainly Roman Catholic, with Northern Ireland, which was mainly Protestant. Occasional incidents took place in the 1950s and early 1960s, but the small amount of support from the Catholics in the largely Protestant Northern Ireland, meant that these efforts became futile. The situation became very different in the late 1960s, when the Northern Ireland Civil Rights Movement started a campaign to protest against discrimination in housing, voting, and employment by the Protestants, or Protestant Ascendancy (Arthur & Cowell-Meyers, 2019). Violence inflicted on demonstrators by extremists, which was not in any way quelled by the largely Protestant police force, would result in a series of attacks that increased in severity on both sides. IRA units were organized to help defend the Catholic community in Northern Ireland. Future Prime Minister Charles Haughey, and another member of the Fianna Fáil government, were tried in Ireland for transporting arms for the IRA. However, they were acquitted of the charges.

Soon, disagreements over the continued use of violence created another rift within the IRA. After a Dublin-based Sinn Féin conference in 1969, the IRA split into the Official and the Provisional wings. Both factions remained committed to a united Irish republic, but the way in which they wanted to achieve that differed. The Officials opted for parliamentary tactics, and after 1972, wanted nothing to do with violent means. While the Provisionals, also known as the Provos, felt that violence was the only way to get rid of the British.

In 1970, the Provos began to carry out bombings, ambushes, and assassinations. This formed part of a campaign they referred to as the "Long War." These attacks were expanded in 1973, and terror ensued in Britain and then throughout Europe. Between 1969—94, it is estimated that the IRA killed approximately 1,800 people, including at least 600 civilians.

The IRA's successes were cyclical in nature post 1970. Britain's policy of imprisoning suspected IRA members and the slaughter of 13 Catholic protesters on Jan. 30, 1972, which was known as Bloody Sunday, encouraged sympathy for Catholic people and the IRA, which helped to swell their ranks.

In the late 1970s, when support for the IRA began to decline, the organization decided to restructure into separate cells, in order to protect themselves against undercover agents infiltrating the organization. By using the assistance from Irish-American groups, the IRA purchased weapons from foreign countries and arms dealers, including Libya. By the late 1990s, it was estimated that the IRA had sufficient weaponry to proceed with its campaign for another 10 years, at minimum. The IRA became especially skilled at fundraising within Northern Ireland by means of racketeering, extortion, and several other illegal activities. It also policed its own community by using punishments, such as beatings and mock trials. Despite the IRA having what might be considered a worthy goal, it is interesting to note how their tactics veered very far into the lane of organized crime. In fact, we can safely say, if they did not have the ultimate goal of achieving independence for Ireland to back them up, their tactics may well have had them classed as any other organized crime group.

It's also important to remember that the IRA trained their members significantly, so otherwise ordinary Irish people were gaining the skills and knowledge it took to run a highly organized secret organization. There can be no doubt that these skills eventually would have spilled over into plainly criminal activities at some point.

In 1981, when 10 political prisoners, including seven IRA members, died during hunger strikes, the political slant of the struggle for independence soon began to overwhelm the military one. It is at this time that Sinn Féin would begin to play a more prominent role. Leaders of Sinn Féin, Martin McGuinness and Gerry Adams, along with John Hume, who headed up the Social Democratic and Labour Party (SDLP), tried to find ways to bring the armed struggle to an end, and thereby filter republicans into Irish democrat politics.

In August 1994, having been promised that a ceasefire would be rewarded by the implementation of multi-party talks, by both the Irish and British governments, the IRA leadership declared that they would be completely ceasing all military activities. In October, a similar promise was made by loyalist paramilitary groups who were fighting to keep in place the Northern Ireland union with Britain. Sinn Féin members, however, were continually excluded from talks, due to the unionist demands for the IRA to disarm, which was a condition of Sinn Féin's being allowed to participate. The ceasefire with the Provisional IRA came to an abrupt halt in February 1996, when a bomb exploded in Docklands, London, killing two people. However, the ceasefire was reimplemented in July of the next year. An agreement was made that disarmament would take place as part of the conflict resolution. IRA's political representatives committed to upholding nonviolent principles, and after this, they were included in the multi-party talks, which took place in the beginning of September 1997.

The Good Friday, or Belfast Agreement, was approved by participants in April 1998. The agreement linked the disarming of the IRA and other steps with a new power-sharing government in Northern Ireland. One of the most important parts of the agreement was that the republicans conceded that the province could remain part of Britain, until the majority of its citizens decided they wished otherwise. This undermined the necessity of continued violent action by the IRA. The IRA did destroy some of its arms stash, but it resisted destroying its entire armory, thereby delaying the carrying out of important sections of the peace agreement. However, in 2005, the IRA made it known that it had brought its armed campaign to an end and they would instead begin to pursue only peaceful options to achieve its aims. In 2015, the IRA made headlines again when it was revealed after a murder investigation, where the victim was a former IRA leader, and that a good portion of the Provisional IRA's organizational structure still existed.

Sinn Féin is an Irish republican and democratic socialist political party active throughout both the Republic of Ireland and Northern Ireland. The name Sinn Féin, in Irish means, "We Ourselves," or "Ourselves Alone." This political party was long believed to be the political wing of the Provisional IRA, but during the 1990s, both the IRA and Sinn Féin went to great lengths to prove their separation. Sinn Féin strove to bring an end to the political separation of Ireland. The party embodied the ideology that varied between republicanism and nationalism, and also advocated for democratic socialism. However, some members of the public questioned how accurately they represented this, due to being a party from the radical left. Gerry Adams led Sinn Féin from 1983 to 2018. He had significant links to the Provisional IRA, even having been in a leadership position in that organization at one point. This fact made it more difficult for the public at large to believe that there was true separation between the two organizations.

Sinn Féin's early history is closely attached to Arthur Griffith, who was the leader of Cumann na nGaedheal or the "Party of the Irish." In 1902, at a meeting in Dublin, Griffith's policy of Sinn Féin, was adopted by Cumann na nGaedheal. This included passively resisting the British, the establishment of an Irish independent local court and ruling council, and withholding of taxes from the British.

Sinn Féin didn't play much of a role until 1916, when the Easter Rising took place. After this, the group became the focal point for the extreme nationalist sentiment, which would be referred to as Republicanism. In 1918, the party won 73 of the 105 Irish parliamentary seats in the British sitting. This win was undoubtedly due to the demand by Eamon de Valera, for an independent and united Ireland, which was a hugely popular standpoint in public opinion. Members of parliament belonging to Sinn Féin met in 1919, in Dublin, and declared that they were a parliament of the Irish Republic. They went about arranging themselves into a provisional government with which they hoped to rival Ireland's British administration.

In 1926, a dispute occurred about how Sinn Féin would participate in the elections for the Dáil. After this, de Valera resigned as leader and went on to found the Fianna Fáil party. Fianna Fáil absorbed most of Sinn Féin's original members. In 1927, during the election held, Sinn Féin acquired less than three percent of the seats and they did not launch a campaign again until 1957. In that election, the group won even fewer seats, and the party turned down the opportunity to occupy them.

In 1969, after a party conference, Sinn Féin split again, due to a conflict in opinion over the IRA's violence.

Even though Sinn Féin was a registered party in Ireland, they were banned in the United Kingdom until 1974. Many leaders within the party were believed to be IRA members, and as a result, the party was issued with broadcasting bans and expulsion orders. Sinn Féin began to emphasize parliamentary and political tactics. In 1981, Sinn Féin took the decision to occupy the seats it had earned in local councils in Northern Ireland. When IRA hunger striker Bobby Sands was elected to the British Parliament, the popularity of republicanism was demonstrated. During the 1982 elections for the Northern Ireland Assembly, Sinn Féin gained close to 11 percent of votes. This was a level of support they managed to retain for the most part.

In 1983, Sinn Féin elected Gerry Adams as their president.

In 1986, Sinn Féin opted to take the seats it won, but the party continued to refuse to participate in the British Parliament. In the following year, the party started having often secret negotiations with the leader of the Social Democratic and Labour Party, John Hume. This party was Sinn Féin's main rival in the area of Irish nationalism, and a few years later, Hume and Adams issued a combined statement of principles in aid of a peaceful settlement to the Northern Ireland conflict. Despite the statement representing Sinn Féin in a different light, the party would continue to be linked with high-profile violence. Adams was given permission by the U.S. President Bill Clinton to visit the country. This decision provided encouragement to the IRA to embark on a ceasefire later in that same year. Sinn Féin was eventually allowed to form a branch in America, called the Friends of Sinn Féin. They were also granted permission to fundraise there. This permission was granted on the belief that the party was committed to furthering nonviolence and democracy. After the IRA reissued a ceasefire, Sinn Féin was allowed to join in on the multi-party peace talks.

After the passing of the Belfast Agreement, elections saw Sinn Féin taking more than 17 percent of the vote and being allocated

18 seats. The Belfast Agreement has also been known as the Good Friday Agreement, as it was passed on Good Friday, April 10, 1998. The agreement was between the British and Irish governments, and most of the political parties in Northern Ireland, on how Northern Ireland should be governed.

Sinn Féin's participation in the Executive Committee was hampered by conflicts over the extent and timing of the IRA disarmament. In 2000, the IRA agreed to allow inspection of its arms dumps by international bodies. This cleared the way for Sinn Féin's total inclusion in the Executive Committee, and it was granted permission by the British government in June of that year. Sinn Féin was the fourth largest party and held two ministerial posts within the Executive Committee.

Participation by Sinn Féin in the political arena increased its support among the Roman Catholics in Northern Ireland. Many of these people were becoming impatient with the slow pace of political change. As a result, Sinn Féin was able to secure more votes and seats in parliament than the Social Democratic and Labour Party. Its members in Parliament, however, refused to take the required oath of allegiance to the British monarch, and thus were not allowed to take their seats. Sinn Féin had its results in the 2002 elections in the Republic of Ireland. They won almost seven percent of the first preference vote as well as five seats.

In 2011, Sinn Féin used the dissatisfied supporters of the ruling Fianna Fáil party, and were able to run a very strong campaign in the general elections in that year. The party's fortunes were additionally buoyed by Adams's choice to campaign, for the first time, for a seat in the south. Adams easily won, and Sinn Féin was able to capture 14 seats.

Before the election in 2017, McGuinness resigned as deputy first minister. He was ill and passed away in March 2017. Michelle O'Neill replaced McGuinness as Sinn Féin's leader in the assembly. In 2018, Adams announced that he would be relinquishing his role as president. His position was taken by Mary Lou McDonald, and she would go on to lead the party to a monumental victory in the 2020 national election, in which the group finished with the highest total of votes and obtained 37 seats.

All counties of the Republic of Ireland have significant Sinn Féin representation. The party is very well-organized locally. At the Ard Fheis, or Annual Conference Party, members from all the local branches debate party policy and elect officers. Regular business for the party is controlled by the Ard Chomhairle, or Central Committee. They meet monthly and are made up of party officers. Nine members are also selected at the Ard Fheis, of which at least one-quarter must be female. The large majority of Sinn Féin's members are young (Arthur, n.d.).

The previously mentioned NORAID was an organization of Irish-Americans established in 1969, after the beginning of Northern Ireland's Troubles. NORAID has as its mission the aiding of the creation of a unified Ireland. This aim is set in the context of the 1916 Easter Treaty. NORAID was known for raising funds for the Provisional IRA during the Troubles, along with other nationalist groups. NORAID circulates a newsletter referred to as, *The Irish People*. The newsletter provides coverage and analysis of events in Northern Ireland.

NORAID was directed and organized by Michael Flannery. In the 1920s, Flannery was a member of the North Tipperary IRA Brigade.

Many different countries and politicians have, at various times, accused NORAID of being nothing more than a front for the Provisional IRA. Allegations were also made that it aided in fundraising for IRA armaments, which were imported from North America in the early 1970s. These accusations have consistently been denied. Former leader of NORAID, Martin Galvin, was banned from entering the United Kingdom in the 1980s.

NORAID was made up of a loose conglomeration of local

branches centered around fundraising by the late 1980s. By the end of 1988, NORAID attempted to expand its appeal, and Sinn Féin sent one of their organizers to the U.S. so more money and time could be devoted to propaganda and lobbying.

A letter would be published in two of New York's Irish weekly newspapers, which claimed that NORAID was being led away from its humanitarian objectives and toward more political goals. One of the letter's signatories was Michael Flannerly, who had quietly resigned from NORAID some time before. Galvin had joined NORAID in the 1970s, and would become the editor of its weekly newspaper and publicity director. Galvin was later appointed to NORAID's board. In the mid-1990s Galvin had split from Sinn Féin, due to the direction that the peace process in Northern Ireland was taking.

In the past, NORAID has supported Project Children, which is a New York-based foundation opened in 1975 that gives children from Northern Ireland summer vacations away from the violence in their home country (NORAID, 2019). Today, NORAID is highly supportive of Sinn Féin.

5

ULSTER

I n this chapter, we'll discuss some of the other organizations that sprang up and were active during the fight for indepen- dence in Ireland. Many of these groups, as was the case with some of the organizations discussed in the previous chapter, had links to organized crime, which in many cases was only justified through their end goal of independence.

The Troubles, which in Gaelic were called Na Trioblóidí, were a Northern Irish ethnic-nationalist conflict that occurred from the late 1960s to 1998. The Troubles were also referred to in the international realm as the Northern Ireland Conflict, and was sometimes called an irregular or low-level war. The Good Friday Agreement of 1998 officially brought the Troubles to an end. The division unofficially would live on, but with less acts of violence.

Despite the geographical focus of the Troubles mainly being Northern Ireland, violence would often leak into other surrounding areas, including England, the Republic of Ireland, and Europe. The nature of the conflict was mostly nationalistic and political and, of course, intensely fueled by historical events. The Troubles also had a sectarian or ethnic dimension, but even though we often divide the conflict up into Protestant and Catholic sides, it actually had very little to do with religion. Protestants and Catholics were not up against each other due to anything their respective religions dictated. Rather, it was due to what history had taught them the other group represented, and a massive number of historic challenges that had resulted in the two groups being opposed.

A major issue in question, of course, was Northern Ireland's status. Loyalists and unionists, who historically were mostly Ulster Protestants, desired that Northern Ireland remain a part of the United Kingdom. On the other hand, Irish republicans and nationalists, largely Irish Catholics, preferred that Northern Ireland not to remain as part of the U.K., and instead, wanted Ireland to be unified.

For the most part, the starting point of the conflict was a campaign launched by the Northern Ireland Civil Rights Association, which hoped to end Protestant Ascendancy. These protests were suppressed by the government. Almost all of the police were Protestants, which resulted in a lot of police brutality against protesters. Loyalists were also very much against the campaign. They said it was a front for the republicans. In August 1969, mounting tensions crescendoed in riots and British troops were deployed. This would become the British Army's longest period of deployment in history. In some areas, peace walls were erected to keep Catholics and Protestants apart. Some members of the Catholic community initially welcomed the British Army. They felt that they were a more neutral force, but they soon realized that the army was biased and hostile, especially after the 1972 Bloody Sunday (Wikipedia Contributors, 2019).

There were two main Ulster organizations involved in the fight against the unification of Ireland: the Ulster Defense Association (UDA), and the Ulster Volunteer Force (UVF).

The UDA was a loyalist organization started in 1971, in Northern Ireland, to arrange the various Protestant vigilante groups' efforts within the province's sectarian conflict.

The UDA was based, at first, in Shankill Road, Belfast. The group was responsible for the politically-motivated murders of Catholics and some prominent republicans' responsibility for most murders was claimed under a pseudonym, the Ulster Freedom Fighters.

In 1992, the British government banned the UDA. Two years later, in response to the IRA's claim to be completely ceasing any violent activity, the UDA combined with other loyalist organizations and declared a ceasefire. However, occasional violence would continue for the first part of the 21st century. In 2007, the UDA publicly announced that they were turning away from violence and also disarmed. In 2010, observers said that the organization's weapons had indeed been decommissioned.

In the 1970s, when the UDA was at the height of its power, it alleged that it had up to 40,000 members and portrayed itself as both a fundraising organization and a paramilitary force. The organization did use legal activities to further its cause, but it was also known for using criminal activities, such as racketeering, to raise funds.

A political think tank was established in 1978 by the UDA. The think tank was called the New Ulster Political Research Group, and its aim was to advocate for Northern Ireland's independence. This, of course, was a policy at odds with mainstream unionism. The UDA was publicly skeptical of traditional unionist politicians. As such, it purposefully separated itself from parliament by means of its staunchly working-class identity. In 1981, the UDA would eventually create its own political party, called the Ulster Loyalist Democratic Party (ULDP).

The ULDP campaigned for a provincial parliament, which

would more fairly distribute power within the U.K. They also called for a bill of rights, as well as amnesty for political prisoners. In 1989, the UDA changed its name to the Ulster Democratic Party (UDP), and it was led by Gary McMichael. McMichael's own father had been a UDA member who was murdered for his political stance. The UDP had earned enough of the electoral vote to be able to participate in multi-party peace talks, which would lead to the Good Friday Agreement. It did not, however, secure any seats in the following elections, and in 2001, it disbanded (Britannica, n.d.).

The Ulster Volunteer Force (UVF), was a protestant paramilitary organization started in 1966, in Northern Ireland. The name of the group was taken from a group of Protestants who had organized in 1912, to stand against Irish Home Rule. The group's most well known leader was Augustus (Gusty) Spence. In 1977, the UVF aligned itself with the Progressive Unionist Party (PUP) after the party was founded.

As the UVF was dedicated to upholding the union between Northern Ireland and Britain, they announced their intention to murder members of the IRA, and they upheld this commitment. The UVF was also responsible for murdering unaffiliated Protestants, Catholics, and members of its own paramilitary group, if they stepped out of line.

The UVF was vulnerable to informants and prone to infiltration and, as a result, its members were often arrested and imprisoned. For instance, in 1977, 26 members of the UVF were sentenced to a total of 700 years in prison for murder and other crimes. In 1979, yet another 11 members were found guilty of killing 19 Catholics.

After 1994, the UVF joined in with the ceasefire, along with the UDA and the IRA, but disagreement within the group caused a split, and the Loyalist Volunteer Force was formed. The Loyalist Volunteer Force then began its own campaign of violence. In May

2007, the UVF denounced this violence and made a pledge to end its armed campaign.

During the 1990s, the Progressive Unionist Party (PUP) once again became popular as a political voice for the UVF. They represented working-class union supporters and political prisoners (Arthur & Cowell-Meyers, n.d.).

6

GANGS AND CRIMINAL ACTIVITY

O rganized crime groups so often operate in the shadows. They are known within their own spheres, and their crimes are seldom publicly claimed. Of course, if a crime is a message from one group to another, the recipient knows very well who the sender is, but for the public, it can be confusing to separate the myth and legend from the reality. In this chapter, we explore some of the most infamous crimes committed by Irish organized crime groups.

Although we'll get deeper into the Westies in the next chapter, it seems fitting to start this chapter with one of their crimes, as they were most certainly of the most bloodthirsty Irish-American gangs, especially when they were engaged in conflict with the Italian Mafia.

The Westies were so dubbed by the media, and, for the most part, they didn't use this name among themselves. The name came from the fact that most of the members (or their ancestors) originated from West Dublin, and they identified with this area.

In fact, in a single day in 1980, the Westies almost succeeded in completely wiping out the New York Italian Mafia. The gang had developed a reputation for being extremely violent and the Gambino family, who led the Italian Mafia in New York, had a lot of respect for the group. Police often wire-tapped both mafia and Irish-American gang phone lines, and infamously members of the Gambino family were heard talking about the Westies, saying, "These guys are (expletive) crazy!" Coming from one of the most infamous Italian-American mafia groups in history, that was high praise indeed. In the 1980s, Paul Castellano, the head of the Gambino family, asked Westies head, Jimmy Coonan, to meet him in a restaurant. Castellano wanted to find a way to reel in the gang a bit so they didn't call too much attention to the underworld.

However, Castellano may not have really known what he was up against. Coonan had many murders under his belt, and he also did not trust the Italians. He attended the meeting, but brought his top enforcer, Mickey Featherstone, with him. Coonan had also assembled a team of his gang members and they waited near the restaurant. Their orders were to move into the restaurant and kill every single person in it, if Coonan and Featherstone did not emerge within two hours.

At the beginning of the meeting, Castellano questioned Coonan about the recent murder of an Italian loan shark. Coonan lied and denied any involvement in the crime. Castellano seemed to accept this, and then started to suggest to Coonan that they start to work more under the radar and not be quite as violent as they had been. If they did, Castellano said the Westies could go under the protection of the Italian mob. Coonan realized that this could help him to increase his power, as well as the profits he was earning. A deal was therefore struck that would entitle the mafia to a portion of the Westies' profit. For this, the Westies would be protected by the Italian Mafia and receive a portion of their business, too.

With the negotiations done, the table of organized crime leaders began to drink and eat. As the minutes ticked by, Coonan suddenly realized that his gang of men would be entering the restaurant at any moment to slaughter everyone present. He quickly excused himself and walked out of the venue to the nearby building where his men were gathered. The gang members were drinking whisky with their guns in hand. Coonan asked why they hadn't yet carried out his orders, and they told him that they thought it best to wait another minute or two and have a whisky for the road (Seamus Hanratty, 2019).

That day, the future of the Italian mob was saved by a single whisky.

The types of crimes that various gangs in America and Canada carried out differed significantly, to the point that police could often tell which organized crime group was involved, just from the modus operandi. The French gangs, for instance, had very little finesse in their crimes. If they carried out a robbery, they would go into the place shooting. The Irish, on the other hand, carefully planned out their crimes. They would spend entire weekends tunneling into banks, rather than going in through the front door and creating chaos. The Irish gangs also had many specialists on their books who were able to, for instance, easily open safety deposit boxes. Even in the early years of the Italian mob, their crimes were often focused on the drug trade. They started with heroin, and then moved on to cocaine.

In Canada, Irish organized crime groups controlled the Port of Montreal for many years, and any drugs that came into Montreal were controlled by them. The Irish Canadian gangs would work with the biker gangs and American Italian Mafia to allow their drug shipments through the port. The Irish, of course, would take a percentage of the drug value as payment for using their port. The heyday for this type of crime in Canada was the 1970s, but today, Irish Turks still run much of that trade (Watchmojo.com, 2011).

One of the more horrific organized crime murders in Ireland took place as recently as 2020. Many of the murders committed by organized crime groups are carried out as a result of a feud or as reprisal for another crime. The murder of 17-year-old Keane Mulready-Woods was one such crime, but its brutality would send a very strong message.

Gang feuds in Ireland have taken the lives of at least 26 people in the last few years, and when the leader of a large local gang lost his best friend, Richard Carberry, to a hit, he decided to take the bloodiest of revenges. Carberry was killed in November 2019, outside his home in County Meath. Carberry's mobster friend, who remains unnamed, hired a hitman to exact revenge. The hitman in question is believed to be responsible for several murders. One such crime committed by the same hitman was the murder of Kenneth Finn in 2018. Finn also worked for a rival gang in Drogheda, which is run by Owen Maguire. Maguire was paralyzed in 2018, after being shot six times.

Mulready-Woods was abducted off the streets, taken to a local home, tortured, and murdered. His murder, and subsequent dismemberment was recorded on video. Mulready-Woods's remains were partially dumped in a sports bag on the street, and his torso is believed to have been sent to the leader of the crime group he worked for.

In 2017, the founder of an Irish-American street gang, which had been involved in trafficking methamphetamine since the early 2000s, received a 100-year prison sentence.

Coby Phillips, a 43-year-old gang member, told the media he had no qualms about his sentence. Part of his conviction was for the murder of an Aryan Brotherhood drug dealer, Darryl Grockett, who had been shot in 2004.

The prosecutor on Phillips's case described it as the most complex case he had ever worked on in his career. Phillips's court case was tumultuous and involved Mexican drug dealers, the infamous Sureño Gang, policemen on the take, and the Irish-American gang—the Family Affiliated Irish Mafia. Phillips founded the gang with three others in the 1990s.

In early 2000, Phillips helped to form a large methamphetamine trafficking ring, which generated hundreds of thousands of dollars each year. The profits were laundered into expensive cars, exotic pets, and mansions. Phillips allegedly even had two alligators imported from Florida to add to his collection. The murder is believed to have taken place because Grocket was planning on robbing two associates of Phillips. These were two Mexican men who were supplying drugs from Mexico through Phillips's network. On the night that Grocket was killed, Phillips had eaten dinner with one of the Mexican men before meeting with the victim. Grocket's body was discovered later that same evening. He had been shot once in the mouth, then the shooter had stood over his body and shot multiple bullets into his chest.

The aforementioned trial was actually the second time that Phillips had been tried for Grocket's murder. In 2013, the jury in his trial for the same crime remained hung. The issue in that trial was a crooked police officer, who had aided the Mexican cartel in their drug dealings. As a result, his testimony in the trial was not accepted.

One of the members of the Mexican cartel that Phillips was involved with was also convicted of the murder, but on a second-degree murder charge.

Another interesting connection with Irish organized crime would happen in Morocco. The Noffel Clan was a Moroccan criminal organization that was started by Naoufal Fassih. After operating in the country of his birth for many years, Fassih went to live in Spain with his cousin, Abdelhadi Yaqout. Yaqout was, by that time, already one of the richest people in Marbella. When Naoufal arrived in Spain, he became friendly with the Taghi Organization, as well as members of the Martha Organization and the Irish mob. This alliance was quite tactical in that he wanted their assistance in assassinating his rival, drug lord Samir Bouyakhrichan. In 2014, Fassih was able to achieve this with the help of members of the

Irish mob, and he became closely connected with the Irish. Fassih was then spending more time in Ireland than he was in Spain. His alliance with the Kinahan Clan became so close that they even used the same hideouts. When Fassih was eventually arrested, he was hiding out in the apartment of a Kinahan member in Dublin (Wikipedia Contributor, 2022).

7

EARLY MOBSTERS & THE WESTIES

Having focused almost solely on groups until this point, we will now start to take a look at some of the individuals who played a major role in Irish organized crime. Some of these individuals are well known, and others may be less so, but they all played interesting and, often, pivotal roles in the development of Irish organized crime across the world and throughout time.

Perhaps the first-ever Irish organized criminal in history was actually a woman. The Pirate Queen, whose real name was Grace O' Malley, lived between 1530 and 1603. She was a sea pirate and became so notorious that Queen Elizabeth I is said to have summoned her to the palace to meet with her. A broadway show called *The Pirate Queen* was based on O' Malley's life.

In the 1700s, after O'Malley, Irish highwayman James Freney ruled the organized crime realm. Freney's family in Ireland lost their land to the English, and he alleged that his robberies and other crimes were his way of getting revenge. Freney was pursued all over Ireland, and eventually, he fled into exile, where he died in 1788.

Billy the Kid is a name that has become synonymous with legend and fables, but the man was, in fact, very real, and he was Irish, too. The Kid's real name was William McCarty, and he was certainly one of the greatest legends of the Wild West. McCarty's parents were some of the earliest immigrants from Ireland to America, in the mid 1800s. His father passed away quite soon after they moved to America, and McCarty was raised by his mother in a New York slum, before the pair headed out West where the Kid's criminal legend would be born.

McCarty was also sometimes known by the alias William H. Bonney. After moving out West, McCarty became a gunfighter and outlaw. He fought in New Mexico's Lincoln County War, and committed three murders during this time. He would then go on to kill another eight men, before he was shot and killed at the age of 21.

In the years that followed, legends grew, which claimed that McCarty had not been killed, and that his death had been staged so McCarty could evade the law. Over the next 50 years, quite a few men came forward claiming to be Billy the Kid. Most of these claims were quickly proven false, but have continued to be topics of debate and discussion throughout the years.

Emmett Dalton, who lived from 1871 to 1937, was the founder of the Dalton Gang. The gang was known as the Wild Bunch, and were one of the most infamous train-robber gangs in the history of the Wild West. The Daltons were first generation Irish immigrants. Emmett was the sole survivor out of his entire gang after they got involved in a shootout with law enforcement, in 1892.

Another legendary criminal Irish-American was Jack Moran, who was known as John 'Legs' Diamond. Moran shot to infamy during the Prohibition Era (1920—1933), when he was known for bootlegging and general gangster crimes. Moran earned a reputation as being invincible, after surviving many attempts at his life.

Also during the Prohibition, in Manhattan, Owney "The Killer"

Madden led the underworld for a long time. He ran the Cotton Club, and was also a leading boxing promoter during the 1930s. Madden had been born in England, but both his parents were Irish.

Charles Dean O' Banion was born in 1892, in Ireland, and his parents immigrated to America soon after. O' Banion became the main rival to the infamous Al Capone during the vicious bootlegging wars in Chicago, during the 1920s.

Michael Spillane was an Irish immigrant gangster, who would be the last of his kind in the 1920s. He was what was referred to as a "gentleman gangster," which was essentially a criminal who was not violent, and was usually very charming and suave. He was commonly known as Mickey Spillane, and ran the Hell's Kitchen underworld in Manhattan, until his death, when he was succeeded by the Westies gang (Irish Central, n.d.).

We briefly discussed James Coonan and his infamous Westies gang in the previous chapter. The man and his gang played such an enormous role in the evolution of Irish organized crime that a deeper dive is most certainly warranted.

The Westies gang was based in New York City from the 1960s to the 1980s, and were predominantly made up of Irish-Americans. Their crimes most certainly fell within the organized crime bracket. They were involved in drug trafficking, contract killing, and racketeering. In the previous chapter, we discovered how the Westies came to partner with the Italian-American Mafia and thereby completely dominated Hell's Kitchen in Manhattan.

T.J. English, a crime author, wrote that although the Westies' membership never actually totalled any more than about twelve to 20 members, the gang became infamous and would go down in history as the last truly Irish gang in the birthplace of the Irish-American mob. Data from the Federal Bureau of Investigations (FBI) and New York Police Department (NYPD) estimates that the Westies were responsible for between 60 and 100 murders, between 1968 and 1986.

Mickey Spillane stepped into a gap in leadership that he saw in Hell's Kitchen, in the early 1960s. Many gang leaders had fled Hell's Kitchen in the early 1950s to avoid being arrested. Hughie Mulligan, a Queens-based mobster, had been running Hell's Kitchen, and Spillane became his second-in-command, until he eventually assumed leadership.

Spillane's gentleman gangster reputation was cemented when he sent floral arrangements to residents who were sick in the hospital and supplied turkeys to poor families at Thanksgiving. In addition to this, he also ran gambling enterprises, including bookmaking and loansharking. His loansharking endeavors led to him letting the gentleman's veneer slip, when he would assault those who had not paid back their loans. Spillane was also arrested for burglary, but his most famous criminal endeavor was his 'snatch' racket.

Spillane worked his way up in social rankings, when he married Maureen McManus, the daughter of the wealthy McManus family. The McManus family had been running the Midtown Democratic Club from 1905. This union of criminal activity with political clout improved Spillane's gang's ability to influence labor racketeering and union jobs. They were able to move away from the floundering waterfront activities, which had occupied them up until that point, and more into service work and construction jobs throughout New York.

During the 1970s, the Irish mob noticed an increasing threat from the Italian Mafia. The Genovese crime family was seeking to control the Jacob K. Javits Convention Center, which was in the process of being built. The convention center was located in Hell's Kitchen, which was, of course, Spillane's territory, and he was completely against allowing any involvement from the Italian Mafia. Despite the fact that the Italian mob largely outnumbered the Irish, Spillane was able to maintain control of the convention center, as well as Hell's Kitchen. The response from the embarrassed and frustrated Italian mob was to hire a rogue Irish-American hitman named Joseph "Mad Dog" Sullivan to put out a hit on Eddie "the Butcher" Cummiskey, Tom "the Greek" Kapatos, and Tom Devaney, who were three of the top lieutenants in Spillane's organization.

The feud between Jimmy Coonan and Mickey Spillane began when Spillane ordered the kidnapping and pistol-whipping of Coonan's father. Coonan, who was then 18 years old, swore he would take revenge against Spillane. In 1966, Coonan attempted to kill Spillane by firing a machine gun at him and some of his associates, from the top of a building in Hell's Kitchen. Coonan did not wound anyone in this attempt, but Spillane clearly received the message that the young man was not to be trifled with. However, Spillane decided to respond in kind, and beat up Coonan's father, leaving him with a message to control his son. Coonan spent a short period of time in prison for murder and kidnapping. When he was released in 1971 , he picked up his war with the Westies where he had left off.

At this point, Spillane felt Hell's Kitchen was no longer a safe place for him and his family. He decided to move to the working-class Irish immigrant neighborhood of Woodside, in Queens. When Spillane left Hell's Kitchen, he began to lose control of his criminal rackets in that area. Coonan soon took over the leadership of Hell's Kitchen, but some loyalists still saw Spillane as the boss. As far as the New York Commission was concerned, Spillane was still the head of the Irish mob in the area, and that would put the Javits Convention Center under his domain. A top member of the Genovese crime family, Anthony Salerno, intended to get the center for himself, and came to an agreement with Coonan. Salerno told Coonan that if the latter was able to take full leadership of the Irish mob in the area, Salerno would split the construction site profits with him.

In 1977, Roy DeMeo, another rogue enforcer, this time of

Italian descent, carried out a hit on Spillane. The hit was ordered by Jimmy Coonan, as he wanted to oust leadership from Spillane. The assassination of Spillane would benefit DeMeo as well, as then, his crew could also do business with the Westies. DeMeo had first met Coonan after Coonan had killed and dismembered the loanshark Ruby Stein.

After Spillane's murder, Coonan intensified the partnership between the Gambinos and the Westies. Coonan's main alliance within the Gambinos, of course, was Roy DeMeo, who had helped to secure his leadership.

The Westies seemed to be capable of getting out of legal trouble quite easily. In 1979, Coonan was acquitted of the murder of a bartender, Harold Whitehead, and James McElroy, another gang member, was acquitted of murdering a member of the Teamster gang in 1980.

In 1980, both of the leaders of the Westies were imprisoned. Featherstone was convicted of federal counterfeiting, and Coonan for illegal possession of a firearm. Despite this, the Westies' loan-sharking, union shakedowns, and illegal gambling activities continued. When DeMeo was killed, Coonan made a new connection in the Gambino family—Daniel Marino, who was an Italian boss hailing from Brooklyn. Coonan would eventually be in direct contact with John Gotti when Gotti took over leadership of the Gambino Family in 1985. Gotti decided to appoint an official liaison to the Westies—Joe Watts—and the gang would occasionally carry out hits for the Gambinos.

Mickey Featherstone, who was another infamous member of the Westies' leadership was found guilty of murder in 1986, and began to provide the government with information, in the hopes that his conviction would be overturned. Featherstone actually believed that his own gang had intentionally framed him for murder. The intelligence that Featherstone and his wife provided, as well as the recordings they assisted in making, helped to achieve this. In 1986, Featherstone's conviction was overturned. The information the Featherstones provided resulted in Coonan and several other Westies being arrested.

After the arrests, Rudolph Giuliani, a federal prosecutor at the time, announced that Coonan and his associates would be charged with criminal activities that stretched back over 20 years. Featherstone would go on to testify in open court over four weeks. The trial that started in 1987, ended the following year, with all defendants being convicted on most charges. Coonan was handed down a 60-year prison sentence. Other members of the gang were also given long prison sentences. This included McElroy, who got 60 years, and Richard 'Mugsy' Ritter, who got 40 years.

After Coonan's imprisonment, the demographic of Hell's Kitchen began to change. The Irish-American community was slowly being replaced by a more ethnically diverse group. This shift also influenced the types of crimes in the area, and saw a change in leadership in the underworld.

Bosko Radonjich was an American-Serbian who had kicked off his affiliation with the Westies in 1983, by being a low-level associate of Jimmy Coonan's. After Coonan's conviction, and after a brief period of temporary leadership by other Westies, Radonjich became the gang's boss. He was instrumental in fixing the 1986 trial of John Gotti, on racketeering charges.

As a result of his interference with the Gotti trial, Radonjich fled the United States in 1992, to avoid jury tampering charges. U.S. Customs officials arrested him in 1999, in Florida. However, it was found that the main witness, Sammy Gravano, was actually unreliable, and Radonjich was released. Radonjich then returned to his mother country, Serbia, where he ran a nightclub and casino until his death in 2011. The period during which Radonjich ran the Westies was referred to as the Yugo Era. When Radonjich fled the U.S., this era ended, and for at least two decades afterwards, there was hardly any mention of the Westies. However, in 2012, the *New*

York Post published an article in which they claimed that the gang had resurfaced. A nephew of a former Westies member, John Bokun, was allegedly running the gang. The man had been caught smuggling marijuana into the U.S., but he denied any affiliations with the gang (Wikipedia Contributors, 2019b).

8

WINTER HILL GANG

Another major player in the Irish-American organized crime world was the Winter Hill Gang.

The Winter Hill Gang was a name used to describe a loose confederation of members of the organized crime world in Boston, Massachusetts. For the most part, the gang's leadership and members were Irish-American. They were often referred to by the overriding term the Irish mob, despite the fact that many of its most influential and prominent members were Italian.

The organization got its name from the neighborhood in which they were founded—Winter Hill in Somerville, Mass. Some of the gangs most notorious members include Whitey Bulger, Buddy McLean, Howie Winter, Joseph McDonald, Patrick Nee, Stephen Flemmi, and Johnny Martorano. The Winter Hill Gang was most influential from 1965, while they were under the rule of Winter and McLean, after which leadership was taken over, in 1979, by Bulger.

The gang was given its name by *Boston Herald* journalists in the 1970s, but the name was not really used to directly refer to the group. The members of the Winter Hill Gang are believed to have been involved with some typical organized crime activities, but they were best known for fixing horse races and arranging the shipping of weapons to the IRA.

This group's influence on organized crime in Boston, as well as their reaching impact over the ocean into Ireland, definitely warrants a deeper dive into their history. The real influence of the Winter Hill Gang was initiated during what is now known as the Boston Irish Gang War, which was 1961—67, between the Irish gangs. The conflict was predominantly between the biggest gang in the Charlestown area of Boston, the McLaughlin Gang, which was led by Bernie McLaughlin, and the Winter Hill Gang, which at that time was led by James 'Buddy' McLean.

For a number of years, the two gangs had existed together in relative peace, until 1961, when an incident on Labor Day weekend changed everything. During a party at Salisbury Beach, Georgie McLaughlin hit on the girlfriend of Alexander Petricone, Jr., a Winter Hill Gang member. Chaos erupted when the advance was brought to light, and McLaughlin was beaten by members of the Winter Hill Gang until he lost consciousness. He was dumped outside a local hospital. Soon after, McLean received a visit from Bernie McLaughlin, who demanded that he hand over the guilty members of his gang. McLean would not comply. The McLaughlins did not take this refusal lightly and felt they had been insulted. In retaliation, they tried to attach a bomb to McLean's wife's the car. In turn, McLean murdered McLaughlin, in 1961, by shooting him as he was coming out of a bar in Charlestown. This was what started the Boston Irish Gang War.

McLean was assassinated four years later by Steve Hughes, one of the last members of the McLaughlin Gang. At this point, Howie Winter assumed leadership of the Winter Hill Gang. A surviving McLaughlin brother was also shot while waiting for a bus, and a year later, the last two members of the McLaughlin Gang, Steve and Connie Hughes, were killed. This hit was carried out by Frank

Salemme. More than 60 men had lost their lives in Boston by the time the war finally came to an end.

When the Irish Gang war ended, the Winter Hill Gang was believed to be the most prominent Irish mob group in the New England area, but this influence even stretched through New York, as well.

James 'Buddy' McLean led the gang from 1955—65. McLean was known as a formidable street fighter. He had a huge number of injuries from the fights he'd been involved in, including damage to his face, scars on his neck, and a damaged left eye. An acquaintance of McLean's once said that he looked like an angel, but fought like a devil.

McLean had an interesting background. His biological parents were Irish, but he was orphaned at an early age and adopted by a family of Portuguese-Americans. As a teenager, he worked as a longshoreman on Boston's docks, and he became good friends with the future leader of the Teamsters gang, William J. McCarthy. McLean started to slowly build his own criminal organization. People easily followed him, because he had such a good reputation as a fighter and his street smarts.

After McLean's death in 1965, Howard 'Howie' Winter took over leadership of the Winter Hill Gang. Howard was born in 1929, in Boston. His parents were German and Irish. Despite being born in America, both Winter's parents were immigrants, which meant that he, too, suffered the discrimination that was so intense against immigrant families at that time. As with many children of immigrant families, this set Winter on a path where he was happy to do anything at all to work against the system. He did not trust police and saw no other path in life other than criminality.

When he initially became involved in the Winter Hill Gang, he and Joe McDonald were the right-hand men to McLean. Winter's particular criminal specialty was horse race fixing, and during his time with the gang, he brought in huge profits from the racket.

One race resulted in a profit of $140,000. Often, Winter would purchase a horse, have the jockey purposefully lose the race, and then profit by means of a fixed comeback.

When McLean died, he and McDonald ran the various rackets jointly, but Winter had the greatest authority. During his 1979 conviction, Winter was sentenced for horse race fixing. He was released in 1987, but by then Bulger had already taken over leadership of the gang, so he took a back seat and instead moved to St. Louis, Mo. There, he would get into a partnership with gang associate James Mulvey. In 1993, he was arrested for trafficking cocaine. Winter was offered a deal for less time if he agreed to provide information, but he refused to rat on anyone and was sent back to jail. He was released from sentence in 2002, and passed away in 2020, in his home in Massachusetts.

When Winter first went to jail, James 'Whitey' Bulger took over leadership of the Winter Hill Gang. Bulger was born in 1929, in Massachusetts. Both of his parents were working-class Irish immigrants and he spent his childhood in a housing project in South Boston. He got his nickname during childhood, because his hair was white-blonde. Bulger's unruliness was apparent even in his youth. He became involved in a street gang when he was a teenager, and had been arrested several times before he turned 18, on a range of charges including battery, assault, and forgery. During this period, he managed to avoid any sentencing for his crimes, and always seemed to get off with warnings or community service sentences.

In 1948, Bulger decided to join the Air Force. He went on to earn a very sketchy record of service, which included several disciplinaries for matters as serious as rape. Despite this, he managed to be honorably discharged after four years of service. Upon his return to civilian life, Bulger went straight back to his criminality, and he was eventually convicted in 1956, of a string of bank robberies. The robberies had been committed across three states and the FBI had therefore been involved in the investigation. He was sentenced to 20 years, but only served nine years and was released in 1965. When he returned to Boston, Bulger became a hitman and enforcer for mobster Donald Killeen. Then, in the 1970s, he became involved in doing similar work for the Winter Hill Gang. Few would know that in 1975, Bulger had actually agreed to become an informant for the FBI. The FBI agent who received Bulger's intelligence was also the child of Irish parents, which perhaps indicates how the path of criminality was not the only one available to children of immigrant parents. The young FBI agent, John Connolly, had actually grown up in the same neighborhood as Bulger, and he had quite admired both Whitey and his brother, who went on to become a powerful politician. It may well have been this influence that Bulger had over the young Connolly that caused their agent-informant relationship to turn corrupt. Soon, instead of the FBI running Bulger, he was manipulating them.

Bulger should also have been indicted for the horse race fixing charges that saw Winter go to jail, but he used his FBI connections to get out of it. When Bulger took over leadership of the gang, he chose a man named Stephen Flemmi as his second-in-command. Flemmi also had a history of being an FBI informant. Together, they extorted money from loan sharks, book makers, drug dealers, and other criminals in the area. Bulger soon developed a reputation for being ruthless.

Despite heading up the Winter Hill Gang, Bulger continued to provide information to the authorities, and the agents he worked with often meddled in investigations of Bulger's crimes, in order to take them off track or turn a blind eye. By the early 1990s, internal investigations started to reveal how deep the Bulger rot had gotten into the FBI, and an independent team was set up to investigate the man's crimes. In 1995, they were ready to charge Bulger, but he was tipped off by his FBI informants and went on the run. Bulger's main informant, Connolly, would later be convicted of several charges relating to his corruption with Bulger. By this point, the press coverage of Bulger's crimes and his escape was enormous, so Bulger and his girlfriend had to regularly move, in order to stay out of the clutches of the police. They eventually settled in Santa Monica, Calif., where they lived under fake identities as Carol and Charlie Gasko.

They were able to keep this up until 2011, when the FBI restarted its efforts, this time focused on Bulger's girlfriend. They were able to locate the couple within days. Bulger was charged with 19 murders, found guilty of 11 of the murders, and given two consecutive life sentences.

Bulger spent several years being passed from prison to prison, because he was a problem inmate, and in 2018, when he was transferred to a West Virginia prison, he was murdered by a group of inmates (Cunningham & Lehr, n.d.).

Bulger would be, by far, the most notorious leader of the Winter Hill Gang. Many books, a play, a film, and several television documentaries would be produced about his life.

In 1995, when Bulger fled, Kevin Weeks took over leadership of the Winter Hill Gang. He had been a good friend of Bulger's and one of his lieutenants at one point. Weeks was another son of an Irish immigrant family in Boston. He was the fifth of six children and was raised in the Old Colony Housing Project. Weeks's father had been a prize boxer and also trained many up-and-coming fighters. Two of Weeks's brothers would go on to be respected political figures, once again highlighting the fine line that often exists between organized crime and politics.

After graduating from high school in 1974, Weeks went on to work as a bouncer in a nightclub, and it would be here that he would be introduced to the Winter Hill Gang. The club, owned by Kevin O' Neil, was called Triple O's Lounge and it was often frequented by gang members. In 1978, Weeks began to work for

Bulger as his part-time enforcer and chauffeur. Bulger became impressed with Weeks's smart ideas for earning money and he grew to like the young man. He decided to bring him in closer than he ever had with another associate. Weeks began to run a loan-sharking business on the side at the same time. In 1982, Weeks left his job and became a full-time mobster.

Shortly afterwards, Weeks was involved in his first assassination on Bulger's behalf. A former associate of the gang—Edward Halloran—had turned FBI informant and Bulger wanted him taken out. Of course, this was ironic, considering Bulger himself was an informant, but that did not seem to matter. What did matter was keeping up the pretense of being the no-nonsense gang leader. Maintaining this reputation, he sent Weeks to stake out the restaurant where Halloran was dining. Bulger waited around the corner in his car with a masked assassin, and both men had two-way radios. When Halloran left the restaurant, Weeks radioed to Bulger that he was on the move. Bulger drove up to Halloran's car and the masked (and still unidentified) assassin opened fire on Halloran's vehicle. Halloran had a passenger in the car, and although Halloran was injured, only the passenger was killed.

In the 1980s, Weeks assisted Bulger in drug trafficking and the men also set up a racket to extort money from drug dealers. They would call drug dealers to Bulger's home and then claim that they had been paid money to assassinate them (no such hit had been put out). Bulger and Weeks offered the men to spare their lives in exchange for large cash rewards. In a world where anyone can turn on one another in a split second, the drug dealers likely often had no reason to doubt that someone had put out a hit on them and many paid up.

Weeks would later allege that they had very strict rules around selling drugs, which included never selling any drugs which might be administered intravenously, no selling to children, and no selling PCP.

When Bulger fled, Weeks stayed in contact with him and they had several secret meetings during Bulger's years on the run, in New York and Chicago. In 1997, Weeks would discover that both Bulger and Flemmi had been active informants to the FBI throughout his dealings with them. He had been astounded, because he'd had no idea this was happening under his nose. In fact, he refused to believe the claims until he met with former FBI agent John Connolly, who showed him Bulger's informant file.

In 1999, Weeks was arrested on drug charges. He was offered a deal: If he became an informant, then he would get a reduced sentence. At first, Weeks refused to rat on his associates, but after a conversation with a fellow prisoner, he changed his mind. He decided that Bulger had been an informant for 30 years, so informing on him would be justified payback. After much consideration, Weeks agreed to show police the graves of six people who had been killed on Bulger's orders. Weeks also revealed that Bulger's politician brothers had been helping him while he was on the run, going as far as to secure him a fake ID. Weeks then testified against John Connolly, and another policeman who had been involved in helping Bulger. In return, Weeks was given only five years in prison.

In 2005, Weeks was released from prison. He went on to work with *People* journalist Phyllis Karas to publish a book about his life with Flemmi and Bulger. At a book signing, Weeks told those present that he'd actually intended to return to life as a gangster after he was released from prison, but with all the publicity around the book, it was now impossible, and he'd be forced to go straight (Wikipedia Contributor, 2022a).

Other notable associates of the Winter Hill Gang who never quite made it to gang boss status included Stephen Flemmi, Johnny Martorano, Patrick Nee, and Billy Shea.

Stephen Flemmi was born to an Italian father and an Irish mother. His parents were working-class people and when Flemmi was 17, he enlisted in the Army and served two tours in Korea. He earned two medals for valor during his service, and in 1955, he was honorably discharged.

Flemmi would become Whitey Bulger's partner just a week after Bulger was signed on as an FBI informant, and most believe that Bulger specifically selected him, because Flemmi, too, was an informant, although the man would deny this.

Besides Flemmi's criminal activities, he was also known to be a serial adulterer and had a string of affairs throughout his life. In one instance, he had affairs with two sisters from the same family. Bulger ended up killing one of the women, because he believed she knew about Flemmi being an informant. In 1985, Bulger and Flemmi killed another woman Flemmi had been in an affair with. Strangely, this woman was also his step-daughter. She had been killed, because she had been threatening to stop her affair with Flemmi and tell her mother (Flemmi's wife) about them. Bulger, Flemmi, and Weeks lured the young woman to Bulger's house and strangled her, then buried her in the basement. This would be one of the bodies that Weeks would lead police to when he turned informant.

Flemmi and Bulger are also believed to have raped many minor girls during the 1970s and 1980s. The men would allegedly get the girls addicted to drugs, and then use this as a tool to exploit them sexually for years (Wikipedia Contributors, 2022a).

John Martorano was a hitman for the Winter Hill Gang. He admitted to having killed at least 20 people for the gang. Martorano was born in Massachusetts. His father was an Italian immigrant and his mother was from Ireland. He was raised as a strict Catholic and was an altar boy in his local church. Apart from his eventual associates in the Winter Hill Gang, Martorano did not grow up in the projects. He was raised, for the most part, in the suburbs and attended excellent schools. Martorano was a good soccer player and received invitations from colleges to play on their teams, but he did not pick up any of these offers. He would later allege that his own father had also been involved in organized crime, and that he had been told from a young age that as the oldest son in the family, he would have to continue the tradition. After school, Martorano started hanging around with Stephen Flemmi, and by age 25, Martorano was a full-fledged mobster and hitman.

Martorano soon became one of the most notorious hitmen and enforcers in Boston. In the 1979 crackdown due to the horse race fixing charges, Martorano was warned beforehand and was able to flee. He lived for 16 years as a fugitive, although he continued to work as a hitman for the mob. In 1995, Martorano was arrested and agreed to a plea bargain. Martorano had been angry that Flemmi and Bulger made no effort to keep him out of the arrests, despite having made plans for themselves. Perhaps the biggest reason Martorano agreed to the plea deal was because he learned Flemmi and Bulger had given up his location, and that is how police found him. Martorano confessed to multiple murders and received a significantly reduced sentence of 12 years. As part of the deal, when he was released in 2007, he was given a $20,000 check to start afresh.

In an interview he gave in 2008, Martorano claimed he had never enjoyed killing, and he only did it if the reason was good or the money was right (Wikipedia Contributors, 2022a).

Patrick Nee was a notable gunrunner, also connected to Weeks and Bulger. Unlike his peers, Nee did not start his life in America. He was born and lived in Ireland for the early part of his childhood. Of that time in his life, he didn't have the difficult memories that many other immigrants reported. In fact, he would tell a journalist in the latter part of his life that although his family was poor in Ireland, they lived what he felt to be a good life, and never went hungry. When extended family members of the Nees began to emigrate to America, the family made the decision to join them.

Nee's father moved first, and would work in America as a laborer for a year until he was able to get a house, and send money for his wife and children for passage by sea. The Nee family then boarded RMS Britannic, and arrived in Boston where they settled.

At the age of 14, Nee became a member of the Mullens street gang. He recalls how becoming a criminal, to him, was a natural path. It was never a decision he made; it simply felt like a natural transition. As an adult, Nee joined the Marine Corps and served in Vietnam.

Upon his return from Vietnam, his brother was shot dead outside a bar by a man named Kevin Daily. Nee tracked down the man who had killed his brother. He waited outside the man's house and shot him several times. He then kicked him in the face and spat on him. Daily survived the attack and Nee was arrested for trying to murder him. When Daily saw Nee in court, he testified that Nee was not the man who had shot him, and Nee was released. He rejoined the Mullens gang at this point and became involved in a feud with another local gang, the Killeens. At one point, Nee would have the opportunity to assissinate Whitey Bulger, which would have significantly changed the landscape of Irish-American organized crime in Boston, but instead, Nee saw an opportunity, and he arranged for a mediation to be conducted around the hit.

When Bulger was in charge of the Winter Hill Gang, Nee focused on fundraising for the IRA, and also was one of the chief organizers of shipments of guns being sent to Ireland. During this time, Bulger often asked him to stop supplying the IRA. Bulger felt the activity was drawing too much attention to the gang and there was not enough profit in it to warrant the risk.

In 1983, Nee took part in the murder of Arthur Barrett, in South Boston. Barrett was a notorious bank robber, who was believed to have large amounts of valuables and untraceable cash that Nee and his associates wanted. Barrett was closely associated with John Martorano and his brother. The Martorano brothers used their friendship with Barrett to lure him to Nee's house, claiming they had stolen diamonds they wanted him to look at. Of course, when Barrett arrived, what he found was certainly not precious stones. He was forced to show the men where his valuables were, and then he was taken to the basement and shot.

Barrett's body was buried in Nee's cellar. In 1999 and 2003, prosecutors in Boston gave immunity to two of Nee's associates, who were at the scene of Barrett's murder, after they provided information. Although they had sufficient evidence to charge Nee with the murder, attorneys decided not to indict Martorano or Nee. This fueled already simmering suspicions that Nee was an FBI informant.

Nee continued to be an associate of the Winter Hill Gang throughout the years, and in 1984, he masterminded an attempt to transport seven tons of assault rifles to the IRA. Bulger helped to arrange the transport of the guns on a fishing vessel, the *Valhalla*. However, the Irish government received a tip about the shipment and the fishing vessel was intercepted by the Irish Navy.

After the failure of the mission, Bulger ordered the torture and assassination of John McIntyre, who had been a crew member on the *Valhalla*. Bulger had received information that McIntyre had tipped off the authorities. Nee played a role in this murder by bringing McIntyre to the house where he was killed. Nee claimed that he thought they were going to interrogate him and allegedly, only later, discovered that the man's body was buried in a basement.

Nee left Boston and spent several years in hiding after being told by Bulger that the FBI was looking for him. In 1987, he was apprehended and served an 18-month prison sentence.

In 1989, after Nee's release, he decided to sever his ties with Bulger. This had a lot to do with their differing views on Irish republicanism—Bulger was always favoring profit over the cause.

Nee then assembled his own crew and started carrying out armored car robberies, in order to raise funds for the IRA. However, in 1990, he was arrested during a robbery, and was caught wearing a mask and in possession of a machine gun, crimes which carried a mandatory life sentence. Nee was handed down a 37-year sentence, but was released in 2000. Interestingly, federal law prohibits any federal offenders receiving reduced prison time or time off for good behavior, and prosecutors were unable to explain why Nee was given this privilege (Wikipedia Contributor, 2021).

9

BORN INTO CRIME

M any of the individuals we've discussed in the book so far were first generation Irish-Americans. Often, either one or both of their parents had been born in and lived in Ireland for some period of their lives. The difficulty of leaving their home country and the adversities they faced in America, paired with the original strife of the Catholic versus Protestant feud, very often made the children of immigrants anti-establishment. Most Irish immigrant families did not trust anyone who was not either Irish or significantly allied with the Irish cause. As a result, for many of these families, it was a feather in one's cap to do anything that stood up to the system, and this often meant criminal activities.

The deep-seated anger from years of discrimination and strife was not the only inheritance that Irish parents would often pass down to their children. With the difficulty of finding jobs when arriving in America, many had become involved in organized crime as a way to survive and support the cause back home. This often became a family heirloom handed down through the generations.

Of course, as we've already seen, not all children of Irish immigrants went the organized crime route. In a single family, half the children may have been involved in gangs, and the other half became involved in politics or law enforcement, for instance.

In this chapter, we will look at a few more individuals involved in the world of organized crime who had Irish blood running through their veins.

William Colbeck (1871-1930) was a figure in the Irish-American criminal underworld who managed to perfectly straddle both politics and crime. Colbeck was a politician in St. Louis, Mo., as well as an organized crime figure. He was involved in illegal gambling and bootlegging. Colbeck went on to succeed William Egan as head of the gang referred to as Egan's Rats, in the early 1920s.

Colbeck was born in St. Louis, Missouri., but had German and Irish parents. He joined the Egan's Rats bootlegging gang when he was a teenager. Colbeck trained as a plumber, while simultaneously working as a gangster. He joined the U.S. Army, after the outbreak of World War I in April 1918, and served in the 89th Infantry Division. When he returned home in 1919, Colbeck was brought in as the right-hand man to gang leader Willie Egan.

Egan was assassinated in October 1921. He had been in front of his saloon when three men in a car drove past and shot him. Colbeck was present when the shooting occured and Egan whispered the names of the shooters before taking his last breath. Colbeck was now the leader of the gang, and he told members that Egan's murderers were John Doyle, Jimmy Hogan, and Luke Kennedy. All three men belonged to the arch rivals of the Rats—the Hogan Gang. The Hogan Gang was led by Edward Hogan, who was the state beverage inspector in Missouri. Colbeck and the gang retaliated immediately and a gang war began in St. Louis.

During the early years of Prohibition, the Rats gang were in control of most of the illegal bootlegging in St. Louis. They soon also started to add to their bootlegging income with armed robberies of armored cars, banks, and messengers. It is estimated that the Rats stole close to $4 million over five years. Colbeck had a reputation for being ruthless with anyone who was an enemy of the gang, and even its own members.

Colbeck would become the most powerful mobster in St. Louis in the early 1920s. The Maxwelton Club became the headquarters for the gang, and Colbeck often handed out bribes, sold illegal booze, or provided other favors from his favorite spot. Colbeck also stood in the St. Louis Democratic City Committee as the sergeant-at-arms. This gave him a political position within the local government. Colbeck was shot during the gang war, but he survived and successfully led his crew, until a peace negotiation was reached in June 1922. Colbeck did not often go along with his men to carry out jobs, but he also had no concerns about doing the dirty work when he needed to. Colbeck was practically fearless under fire. He had lived through many dangerous years on the streets, as well as in combat, and he was an excellent shot with his weapon of choice—the Browning Automatic Rifle.

The gang war between the Rats and the Hogans began again in February 1923, when six Rats, including Colbeck, carried out a hit on Jacob Mackler, a Hogan Gang lawyer. Once again, regular shootings rocked St. Louis, but on Easter Sunday 1923, both Colbeck and Hogan wrote letters that were published in the St Louis newspapers, announcing to citizens they were halting the gang war permanently.

By 1924, the Rats were the most powerful they had ever been, but trouble was brewing on the horizon. Factions had been developing within the Rats, and Colbeck had ensured that he was surrounded by his four main gunmen: Steve Ryan, bodyguard Louis 'Red' Smith, David Robinson, and Oliver Daugherty. Some of the Rats members had fled town and others had gotten on Colbeck's bad side. In one event that displayed the severity of the problems within the gang, Colbeck and his four men assassinated a gang member who had been talking about them behind their backs at the Maxwelton Club.

By this time, the police were also closing in on the Rats. Colbeck and two of his top men were tried for two robberies. In one of these robberies, the gang got nearly $2.4 million in negotiable bonds and cash. In order to pay the legal fees that were mounting, Colbeck and some of the gang members robbed the Granite City National Bank in April 1924, which netted them $63,000. It was also believed that Colbeck had ordered an assassination on his longtime friend, Michael Kinney, who was a Missouri State Senator. Kinney, however, survived his injuries, and no one was charged for his attempted murder.

In November 1924, after the damning testimony from a fellow gangster, Colbeck and eight of the rats were convicted and sentenced to 25 years in prison. While Colbeck was in prison, he shared a cell with Al Capone. It's believed that Capone and Colbeck got along so well that they had planned to work together when they were both released. However, this never happened, because Capone was transferred to Alcatraz in 1934.

Colbeck was paroled in November 1940, and claimed that he was going to work as a plumber and would no longer be involved in crime. However, soon Colbeck and some of his old gang members were said to be trying to infiltrate the St. Louis underworld again. In February 1943, Colbeck was found shot to death in his vehicle. The motive for his assassination seemed unclear, but he may have been the target of crime bosses who didn't want him getting back into the scene, or perhaps for a long-held grudge. No one was ever charged for Colbeck's murder (Wikipedia Contributors, 2021).

Vincent Coll, who was born as Uinseann Ó Colla, was an Irish-American hitman for the mob, from the 1920s until the early 1930s, in New York. Coll became infamous for allegedly accidentally killing a young child during a kidnapping attempt.

Coll was born in Ireland and was related to the infamous Curran family. The Coll family moved to the United States in 1909. Coll also was distantly related to Bríd Rodgers, a former Northern Ireland Assemblywoman.

When Coll was 12, he did his first stint in a reform school. After that he was expelled from many different Catholic reform schools, and he eventually joined the Gophers gang. Coll quickly gained a reputation for being a wild young boy. When he was 16, he was detained for being in the possession of a gun, and by the time he was 23, he had 12 arrests to his name. In the late 1920s, Coll started working as an armed guard for Dutch Schultz's mob. Schultz was running a bootlegging business and Coll guarded the delivery vans.

The fact that Coll was known to be ruthless made him a valuable enforcer to Schultz. During the 1920s, Schultz's empire began to grow, so he decided to move Coll from his armed guard position to one as an active assassin. Coll was just 19 when he was charged with murdering Anthony Borello and Mary Smith. Borella owned a speakeasy and Smith ran a dance hall. Coll was believed to have carried out the murder of Borello, because the man would not sell Schultz's illegal alcohol. Both murder charges were eventually dismissed, and this is believed to be due to Schultz's influence. Coll's boss was not happy with the young man drawing attention in this way though, and the killings had not been mandated by him. In 1929, once again without Schultz's consent, Coll robbed a dairy of $17,000. Coll and some associates posed as guards to get access to the room in which the money was kept. Schultz confronted Coll about the matter, but Coll was not apologetic and, instead, he demanded to be made an equal partner in Schultz's dealings, a demand that was declined by Schultz.

Coll then decided to form his own gang and became engaged in a feud with Schultz. Coll's older brother became one of the first victims of the feud. He was killed in May 1931. After this, Coll became enraged, grief stricken, and intent on seeking vengeance. In the next three weeks, Coll shot four of Schultz's men. In total, at least 20 men lost their lives during the feud. At the same time the vicious Castellammarese War was also going on, so the streets of Manhattan were chaotic, and it was often difficult for police to know which body belonged to which feud. The Castellammarese War was a brutal power struggle in New York City for control of the Italian-American Mafia. The war lasted from February 1930 until April 1931, and was mainly waged between members of Joe "The Boss" Masseria's group and those of Salvatore Maranzano.

Coll then broke into one of Schultz's garages and demolished 10 trucks and 120 of his vending machines. This was an enormous blow to Schultz's businesses. In order to finance his new gang, Coll would often abduct rival gangsters and keep them for ransom. As others who had carried out this 'snatch' racket knew, criminal victims would not report their kidnappings to police. They would also have a tough time explaining why the cash they used to pay ransoms had never been reported as income. One of the most infamous of Coll's victims was professional gambler George DeMange. DeMange was a close friend of Owney Madden, who led the Hell's Kitchen Irish mob. One recounting said that Coll had telephoned DeMange and requested to meet up with him. When DeMange arrived at the arranged location, Coll abducted him at gunpoint. He held the man for 18 hours before releasing him, upon delivery of the ransom.

In July 1931, Coll is alleged to have taken part in an abduction attempt that led to the shooting death of a child. The actual target in this snatch racket was the bootlegger Joseph Rao, who was also a Schultz underling. The man was relaxing in front of a club and a group of children were playing on the street outside a block of apartments across the road. At this point, a car pulled up to the curb, and a group of men in the car pointed large guns at Rao and began firing. Rao flung himself onto the sidewalk, and four of the children were also wounded in the attack. One of the children, a 5-year-old named Michael Vengalli, died of his injuries. After the death of the child, New York City Mayor at the time, Jimmy Walker, called Coll a "mad dog."

In October 1931, After a huge manhunt, police arrested Coll at a hotel. Coll had attempted to disguise his appearance by dying his hair black and growing a mustache. He was also wearing glasses. Coll surrendered without a fight. He refused to answer any of the police questions, and insisted that he hadn't even been in the area of the murder at the time. Despite his insistence, a grand jury indicted Coll for the child's murder.

Coll's trial started in December 1931. He was defended by well-known defense attorney Samuel Leibowitz. Coll continued to claim he was nowhere near the shooting and that he was being framed. He also publicly said that if he found the person who killed Vengalli, he would tear their throat out. Rather quickly, the prosecution's case fell apart. Their only witness to the shooting, a man named George Brecht, was found to have a criminal record and a history of mental illness. He also claimed to have been a witness in another murder case in Missouri, and the general consensus became that he was an attention seeker. As a result of the general lack of evidence, the judge passed down a verdict of not guilty.

After the not guilty verdict was passed down, a New York police detective told Coll that he would be arrested if he was ever spotted in the city. Within a few days, he was rearrested for being in possession of a gun. The arresting officer referred to him as a baby killer, to which Coll angrily responded, "I am no baby killer!" Not long after Coll was acquitted, he married fashion designer Lottie Kreisberger.

Coll was soon hired as an assassin by Salvatore Maranzano. Maranzano had declared himself Capo Di Tutti Capi, or "The Boss of All Bosses," and hired Coll to assassinate Charles Luciano, the acting boss of the mafia. Luciano, however, was warned that there was a hit out on him. Months before, Luciano had brought the infamous Castellammarese War to an end, by having his own boss assassinated. This left Maranzano as the most powerful mafia boss in the five Italian mob families. However, soon Maranzano decided Luciano was also a threat. In September, Maranzano asked Luciano, Frank Costello, and Vito Genovese to his office in Manhattan. Luciano was wary and certain that this was going to be an ambush. So he decided to act first. Luciano instead sent four hitmen who he knew Maranzano would not recognize. The men were disguised as government agents, and two of the men disarmed Maranzano's guards. The other two stabbed Maranzano and shot him.

In 1963, testimony from government witness Joseph Valachi revealed Maranzano had paid $25,000 to Coll to take out all three men who had been invited to his office that day. However, when Coll arrived at the office, he found Maranzano was dead and he fled the building.

It has been alleged that both Owney Madden and Schultz had put a $50,000 target on Coll's head. In one instance, Schultz actually walked into a police station in the Bronx and said he would give a house in Westchester, N.Y., to anyone who killed Coll.

In February 1932, five gunmen burst into Coll's apartment and riddled the place with gunfire. Three of Coll's gangsters were killed, but Coll arrived on the scene half an hour later.

A week later, Coll was on a public phone in a drug store in Manhattan. On the other end of the phone was Owney Madden. Coll was demanding $50,000 from the gangster, or he would kidnap his brother-in-law. Madden held Coll on the line while he had the call traced. While he was on the phone, a dark limousine pulled up outside the drug store with three men inside. One man remained in the car, and the other two stepped out. Of those men, one remained outside the store as a lookout, while the third entered. The gunman told the cashier to keep cool and pulled a submachine gun out from under coat. He fired on the telephone booth in which Coll stood. The infamous assassin died instantly and the killers escaped in the limousine. A chase ensued, but it was unsuccessful and they got away.

Coll had been shot more than 15 times. He was laid to rest beside his brother, whose murder he had so viciously sought vengeance for.

The men who had killed Coll were never identified. Schultz's attorney later claimed that another famous gangster, Bo Weinberg, had been the getaway driver. The gun that killed Coll was confiscated a year later from a Hell's Kitchen assassin named Tommy Protheroe, after he had used it in another murder. In May 1935, in what seemed to be a retribution killing, Protheroe and his girlfriend were murdered by unknown gunmen.

Schultz would run his illegal businesses for only a few more years. In October 1935, he was killed at a restaurant in New Jersey. This hit was allegedly ordered by Luciano in conjunction with the new national crime syndicate.

Coll's widow, Lottie, would also be convicted of being in possession of a concealed weapon, and she was sentenced to six months in jail. Despite being granted parole, Lottie refused to leave prison, because she believed that the same people who had killed Coll were after her.

In 1935, Owney Madden moved to Arkansas, because he still felt the pressure of police scrutiny around Coll's murder. He died there in 1965 (Wikipedia Contributors, 2022a).

Elmer Burke, whose street name was 'Trigger,' was an infamous hitman in the 1940s. Burke was raised by his brother, Charlie, after their parents died. In 1941, Burke was remanded to a reform school, but was later released when he expressed an interest in joining the army. Burke went on to serve in the army in Italy as a Ranger. He would later be imprisoned for two years in Sing Sing Prison, N.Y., on a robbery charge. During this jail stint, his brother, who he idolized, was killed by a man named George Goll. Goll was detained for the crime, but he was later released. In an act of revenge, Burke shot Goll. This murder, and others he would commit, helped him to earn his nickname 'Trigger,' because he had a habit of shooting people behind the ear. It would also be this modus operandi that would link him to other crimes and have police catch up with him. Burke would hold businesses in Manhattan to virtual ransom and force them to pay for his protection.

In 1952, Burke went on to murder Edward Walsh as the man sat in a bar with his friend. Burke shot the man, because he tried to stop Burke from forcing protection money out of the bartender. However, Walsh didn't do this as an act of honor; he was already extorting the bartender himself and didn't want to lose the money to Burke. Earlier that day, Walsh had broken up an argument between the bartender and Burke. Burke left the bar at that time, but returned with his weapon and shot Walsh in the head. At the time, Burke was dating Walsh's sister. Burke was a man of small stature and almost never solved disagreements with physical fights —he always used his gun.

Burke was also involved in what would become known as the Brinks Job. This was a record heist that took place in 1954, in which a group of mobsters hired Burke to kill Joseph O'Keefe. O'Keefe was the brains behind the million-dollar Brinks robbery. The mob believed that O'Keefe was being pressured by police to become an informant.

Burke accepted the job and went to Boston to hunt down O'Keefe. He found the man in a Massachusetts housing project and ran him down for thirty minutes while firing numerous rounds at the man. Burke finally managed to shoot O'Keefe in the leg. Burke believed he had killed O'Keefe, and got into his car and drove away. He stayed in the Boston area for a while after that.

O'Keefe was only wounded and immediately contacted the police and laid a charge of attempted murder against Burke. Burke was detained a week later and held at the Charles Street Jail from where he escaped, before being recaptured a year later.

Burke was tried and convicted of murdering Edward Walsh, as well as the attempted murder of O'Keefe. He was sentenced to death. On Jan. 9, 1958, Burke enjoyed his final meal of steak, he smoked six cigars, and then spent his last night reading newspaper articles about himself. As Burke was placed into the electric chair, he smiled and waved at the gathered crowd.

Edmund Boyle lived in Brooklyn. He was well known for being an innovative money maker and worked well under pressure. In the late 1980s, Boyle became involved with the Gambino crime family. He started off his criminal career with car thefts, and soon became a trusted accomplice of Thomas Carbonaro, who was a Gambino family soldier. Boyle would go on to become trusted and respected by the Gambino family, after participating in many crimes with them, including bank robberies, illegal gambling, murder, and extortion. Boyle assembled his own crew, which was referred to as the Night Drop Crew. Rather than being an organized gang, the group was more like an often-changing assembly of Gambino family associates (Wikipedia Contributors, 2022d).

It was alleged that Boyle's crew had stolen almost $1 million from the National Westminster Bank, in Brooklyn. Their other bank robberies had netted a profit of almost $2 million. The crew was specialized in their crimes. They had developed specific tools that they used for grabbing cash bags, which were deposited in drop chutes by businesses over weekends. The group searched for banks situated in business districts and punched out the drop chutes. They were the only group in the United States operating with this modus operandi. In 1997, four members of the crew targeted a fellow associate named Frank Hydell. They believed Hydell was an informant to the government.

Hydell's brother had gone missing 10 years before. It would emerge that he was abducted by two crooked cops who were working with the Italian Mafia. The policemen delivered Hydell's brother to the Luccese family underboss, who proceeded to torture and kill him. The reason was because the underboss believed the man tried to carry out a hit on him. It was at this point, after discovering that his brother had been murdered, that Frank Hydell started cooperating with the government. As a result, in 1998, Frank Hydell was shot and killed while exiting a club on Staten Island. Boyle was arrested and convicted of conspiring to kill Frank Hydell, although he was found not guilty of actually having committed the murder himself (Forsyth, 2019).

10

PRESENT DAY

Although Irish-American gangs have dwindled significantly, Irish organized crime still has a significant standing both in its motherland and in other countries.

Despite the independence and reunification of Ireland having been the driving force behind much of the organized crime that had its roots in Ireland, today, reunification is still an ongoing question.

At one point, the border between the Republic and Northern Ireland was made up of a wall of barbed wire, which was guarded by heavily armed soldiers, however, today that border is a multi-lane roadway. For non-locals, it's almost impossible to know where the Republic ends and Northern Ireland begins. Despite this, those who fought the battles for independence, and especially those who still advocate for reunification, are all too aware of the division.

Irish nationalists have never given up on the dream of a unified Ireland, but there has never been a clear way to achieve this. However, today, just over 100 years since the split first occurred, reunification may be a realistic possibility. Sinn Féin, which still continues to actively advocate for reunification, has consistently

89

won in the Republic of Ireland's elections and continues to do so. The party has called for a vote across both the Republic and Northern Ireland, in 2025, to decide whether the people want reunification. This revival of the party's original manifesto has, in part, been motivated by Britain's 2020 exit from the European Union (E.U.), which is referred to as Brexit.

Today, although the bulk of its support remains in the Republic, Sinn Féin has representatives in parliament on both sides of the border. In recent elections, the party has, for the most part, campaigned around anti-austerity policies, as well as relief for the increasing homelessness crisis in Ireland.

Although it may not have gained as much focus, while the English were voting for or against Brexit, the Irish also realized that the move would create a turning point for them, too—should they stay in the E.U. or the U.K.? Most in Northern Ireland more closely relate to the E.U., and this connection has almost become a part of Irish identity.

In 2016, Northern Ireland voted to remain part of the E.U., and since then there has been a huge increase in British and Northern Irish residents applying for Irish passports. The closeness many Irish feel to the E.U. is not just a geographical sense. It also comes from the knowledge that for many years during the struggle, funding for the peace process, rebuilding of infrastructure, and trade, came from the E.U. While Brexit was being negotiated, many in Northern Ireland felt that the British government was not taking them into account in their decision-making process. Sinn Féin also highlighted this on many occasions, saying that overall, those in Westminster never had much thought of the impact of their decisions on the Irish, and they believed the government also had very little understanding of how the region would be affected by Brexit.

Logistically, Brexit also means that now, a non-E.U. region (Northern Ireland) borders up against an E.U. member region (the

Republic of Ireland). The border between the regions had been a major point of discussion during the negotiations, because it would not be feasible to return to a hard border. This would only reopen the trauma of the conflict of years gone by and, from a practical perspective, be economically devastating to both sides of the border.

After extended negotiations, English Prime Minister Boris Johnson agreed to have a trade border in the Irish Sea, rather than the land border. This essentially means that the island is unified for the purpose of customs, but remains politically complicated.

With Sinn Féin having been a pariah party for a long time, many political experts find it remarkable that Brexit has seemingly resulted in such a surge of support for the party, presumably because of its unification-based manifesto. Even before unification became a hot topic again, the other two main parties, Fianna Fáil and Fine Gael, began to slowly lose support, simply because they were not focusing on enough of the basic issues like housing and health care that impacted the average Irishman.

While the idea of reunification may be something that many aspire to, the large majority believe that, for now, it is simply a bridge too far. The first step would be a poll, and the logistics of arranging and actioning that also seem to be pie-in-the-sky at this point (Duggan, 2020).

With the Irish conflict all but a thing of the past, and all factions having renounced violence and put down their arms, this has left Irish organized crime in a bit of a quandry.

For a long time, Irish and Irish-American organized crime had a cause to pin its flag on. They were almost Robin Hood-like—taking from the rich to give to the cause of freedom. However, as this cause began to evaporate, it became clear that these gangs and organized cells were more than happy to continue reaping the profits of their crimes regardless.

However, the face of Irish organized crime has changed. Today, as is this case with most organized crime across the world, it is far more drug related. Also, as the world has become a more connected place, Irish organized crime has, too. It has begun to hold hands with some of the most powerful organized crimes groups internationally, in order to expand its reach. In 2021, the *Irish Examiner* reported that major Irish gangs had begun to work with Dutch and Italian organized crime groups, in order to create a cocaine boom across the E.U.

In a report compiled by E.U. and United Nations (U.N.) drug agencies, this increased cooperation between international criminal factions is called a "new phenomenon." In the last few years, Dubai is noted as being the base for the Kinahan Cartel. It is there that the Irish, Bosnian, Dutch, and Italian organized crime groups have assembled to form what has been referred to as a super cartel. The main individuals involved in the cartel are Irishman Daniel Kinahan, Dutchman Ridouan Taghi, Italian Raffaele Imperiale, and Bosnian Edin Gacanin.

The motivation behind the collaboration is a pooling of capital, in order to purchase stock at far lower prices and thereby, maximize profits for everyone. In this way, Irish gangs are able to gain a far greater share of the European cocaine market. The proof of the power behind this collaboration has been seen in the multi-ton seizures being made by law enforcement in the last few years. The cartel works by posting gang representatives in drug source countries (O'Keeffe, 2021).

Back in Ireland, organized crime has maintained, and even heightened its reputation for ruthlessness. As street gangs have become more drug focused, turf wars and retribution feuds have become more common. However, if one takes a wide angled view of the last 20 years of gang crime in Ireland, for instance, an interesting picture emerges.

The beginning of this 20 year period was marked by a decade of significant carnage, then there was a lull in violence for about five years, whereafter, the violence escalated to never before seen extremes.

That first violent period included a major drug seizure in 2000, in a Dublin hotel, as well as the 2010 murder of Eamon Dunne in a pub. During this period, there were extensive gangland feuds with most crimes involving guns. In March 2000, an infamous feud among Irish gangs started, referred to as the Crumlin-Drimnagh feud, and it started over a drug seizure. In January 2003, the Limerick feud was completely unrelated. In a decade, the feud took at least 30 lives. While those two feuds were certainly bloody enough, at the same time, another gang in Finglas, Dublin, which was headed up by Marlo Hyland and Eamon Dunne, also went on a murderous spree, killing at least 11 people in three years.

As we've seen happen with many other trigger-happy gang leaders, Dunne's associates in the underworld were not happy with how much attention his actions were bringing to them, and to return calm, a hit was carried out on Dunne. After Dunne's assassination, a lull of sorts descended on organized crime in Ireland. Of course, all the crimes continued on underneath the reverie, but there were no huge bouts of violence for some time.

In 2015, when Dubliner Gary Hutch was killed in Spain, a second explosion of gang feuds erupted in the Republic, which for the most part continues until today.

Gary Hutch's murder then sparked the so-called Kinahan-Hutch feud, which also represented the first time an international Irish gang, the Kinahans, had been involved in a feud in Ireland. In 2018, between Hutch's murder and the most recently recorded murder related to the feud, 18 people lost their lives to the Kinahan-Hutch conflict. This is the largest number of deaths in any Irish gang feud to date.

One of the attacks in the Kinahan-Hutch feud would strongly hark back to the roots of Irish organized crime, when a team of armed men dressed in fake Garda uniforms and armed with IRA-supplied AK-47s burst into a hotel, in an attempt to target a rival group. Another new development in this feud has been the assassination of so-called 'soft' targets to get at rivals. This means the killing of extended family members related to the core family or their associates. Until now, this type of attack has been a mark of Asian and Latin-American organized crime. Many people in the extended Hutch family were shot dead during this time, with the sole goal of putting pressure on Gerry Hutch.

The feud seemed to calm down a bit in December 2018, but in the months leading up to 2020, another five men were murdered. It seems that with each gang feud that starts up in Ireland, the intensity of the violence increases. Many of the victims in this most recent feud have been very young men, on average between 21 and 23. One of the victims was shot in the head, while pushing his infant son in a stroller. Another was assassinated when he went to the home of another man who had been killed earlier that day (Lally, 2021).

Meanwhile, back in America, an Irish prison gang has reportedly been involved for years in a feud with the Aryan Brotherhood. There have been conflicts between the Irish and right wing groups like the Aryan Brotherhood before, because the group often includes immigrants in its list of people it targets.

In 2016, a shootout left one member of the Brotherhood dead, and the Irish mob desperately trying to keep their lips sealed about what had led to the attack.

The gang operates predominantly from behind bars, and the order to attack the Brotherhood came from an incarcerated ringleader. Details about the attack emerged in court testimony in an Oklahoma trial. In the early hours of Jan. 30, 2016, three Irish mob members burst into an Oklahoma hotel room and fired 29 shots, killing Justin Lucas—a Brotherhood associate. The shooters wore green and white bandanas over their faces. During the feud between these two gangs, the Irish mob had been given orders to kill on sight if they encountered any Brotherhood members. As a reward for any successful assassinations of Brotherhood members, the Irish mob members were allegedly promised up to a half a pound of methamphetamine. The three mob members were charged with first-degree murder and all pleaded not guilty. One of the kingpins of the Irish gang, Richard Coker, is also believed to have offered one of his enforcers heroin, in exchange for killing a witness to the hotel shooting. Another witness was shot in the chest, also allegedly by a mob member, but survived the attack. Coker has directed the activities of the gang, including significant drug sales, from his prison cell.

An FBI agent testifying in the case, said the Irish mob has a history of intimidating witnesses in cases. Also in 2016, police in Tulsa, Oklahoma, arrested two Irish mob members after they had kidnapped a woman and her two children. The woman was thought to be cooperating with police in an investigation into the Irish gang. Although the woman and her children were not harmed, they did threaten their lives if she continued to work with police (Bailey, 2017).

With super cartels being formed and unabated violent feuds occurring all over the world, one must wonder, where will it all end? There are many countries in the world, especially in Latin America, where organized crime runs the country. In these instances, the drug economy has become so dominant that it's almost impossible for government or law enforcement to fight back anymore. In the U.K., some hope that Brexit may help to get organized crime back under control.

In February 2020, when the U.K. ceased to belong to the E.U., the region entered a transition period. For many, this has been a period of uncertainty, but members of government who have vehemently supported Brexit, insist that the change will make the U.K. a safer place to live in, because they will have full control over its borders.

Negotiations continue on exactly how the relationship between the E.U. and the U.K. will be impacted, but it is important to ponder exactly how Brexit will impact the criminal landscape in the region.

Does Brexit present any risks or opportunities for criminal groups? Exactly how does Brexit impact the power of law enforcement to control organized criminal activity in their region?

The fact is, Brexit may indeed make organized crime stronger. With the U.K. leaving the customs union with the E.U., and having more freedom to impose self-determined tariffs on imports—while simultaneously maintaining an open border between the Republic and Northern Ireland—a huge increase in cross-border smuggling is possible. It is possible organized crime groups would make use of the price differences between the U.K. and the E.U., in order to undercut legal imports and avoid customs tariffs.

Some of the smuggling gangs that already work on the border between Northern Ireland and the Republic show how this would be possible. Although import duties were, for the most part, standardized in 1993, tax on items such as alcohol, tobacco, and fuel have continued to differ. Groups in this area have long capitalized on this, and gang activity often involves the smuggling of fuel and counterfeit tobacco products.

Many of the groups that are currently involved in smuggling activities have been historically linked to the struggle for independence. It therefore makes sense that by expanding the group of products for which price differentials exist helps to boost the smuggling market.

In 2019, an inquiry into the smuggling trade on the border said the area was a huge risk and there was a major opportunity for criminal organizations to make significant profit in the region.

However, the more frightening risk is that it is not just the smuggling of goods that could be promoted. Human trafficking may also see a huge increase. While limitations on immigration to the U.K.—especially for lower skilled employment seekers—appears to be much lower under the new Brexit regulations, this may be to the detriment of those people. Work opportunities could diminish and the number of illegal immigrants entering the U.K. could possibly increase, and not all of these people will be entering the region of their own accord. Several human rights organizations have already insisted that the new regulations are going to create an environment where abuse and coercion is common, and the black market for lower-skilled labor will boom.

The border between the Republic and Northern Ireland could become a common place for human trafficking to occur. Both U.K. and Irish law enforcement have already seen Nigerian and Romanian crime organizations using the common travel area as a point for their human trafficking endeavors.

As for the trafficking of illicit drugs, which is the main money maker for criminal organizations, Brexit may aid this also. Currently, the major flow route for drugs into the U.K. is through the E.U. Primarily, Belgium and the Netherlands are the routing points for drugs coming from South America destined for the U.K. In order to control this in the past, E.U. and U.K. authorities have had to work closely, but Brexit may change that and provide criminal groups with an even easier freeflow.

Money laundering may also be far easier in the U.K. for criminal groups post-Brexit, because the region starts to position itself as a hub for foreign investment. Not all of that investment will be legitimate. U.K. businesses that may have depended on E.U. trade for the large portion of their income, will now be looking more closely at non-E.U. countries to supplement their profits. This poses the risk of these businesses finding themselves drawn into corrupt practices. The ease with which it is possible to establish shell companies in the U.K. also adds to the risk that this will happen more frequently.

Clearly, Brexit could present some huge opportunities for criminal organizations, and law enforcement's response will be key. So, how exactly might Brexit impact the way in which U.K. officials are able to respond?

The most basic impact is that the U.K. is losing law enforcement resources by leaving the E.U. As a member of the E.U., a country has access to the European Union's Judicial Cooperation Unit, (Eurojust) and the European Union's law enforcement agency (Europol). Eurojust was set up to help improve and stimulate the coordination of prosecutions and investigations, as well as facilitating cooperation between the relevant authorities in the European Union member states. This cooperation is mainly in relation to serious cross-border crime, including organized crime. Europol offers various services to its member states, including a support center for law enforcement operations, a hub for information about criminal activities, and a center for law enforcement expertise. The types of crimes that Europol helps to combat across the E.U. include terrorism, money laundering, drug trafficking, organized fraud, counterfeiting, and human trafficking.

Although the Brexit agreement does have a provision for the U.K. to still enjoy some form of access to these organizations, it is unclear how this will happen, and the longer it takes to define this, the greater the hold of organized crime increases. The U.K. will most certainly lose active access to the Europol database, and investigations will be slowed if authorities have to submit cases manually on a case-by-case basis.

Just losing access to this database alone is a huge blow, considering U.K. agencies use the Europol databases for 250,000 searches a year, on average. There are also other resources in Europol's cache that are vital to effective law enforcement in a region with such a high number of foreign criminal influence. These include the European Intelligence system, the Secure Information Exchange Network Application, and the European Union

Bomb Data System. This represents a loss of huge amounts of critical information.

The loss of resources for investigations is one thing, but even after a criminal individual or network is identified, Brexit means that arresting criminals who may have fled to other countries becomes much more difficult. The European Arrest Warrant (EAW) provides for the automatic extradition of criminals throughout the E.U. In 2017, approximately 1,735 wanted individuals were surrendered to the U.K. for prosecution on the basis of the EAW. After Brexit, this will no longer be possible.

Increasing connectedness throughout the world has had many benefits, and this is no different for the organized crime community. Irish organized crime groups have linked with international groups and formed strong alliances, and Brexit may play into their favor by increasing their stretch and profits. In the crime community, of course, profits mean power, and we may start to see some of the most powerful gangs, cartels, and groups emerging in the next few years (Stanyard & Tagziria, 2020).

CONCLUSION

Since the first human beings appeared in Ireland, and the first records of their interactions were made, the country has been a place of strife, conflict, and hardship. However, despite this, the Irish identity has held strong, though it would come to mean different things to different people.

There is no doubt that the people of Ireland have been sorely impacted by invasions, land loss, and control by the English. However, it has perhaps been the internal struggle and conflict among its own people that has set the rhythm for the history of the Emerald Isle.

The conflict and separation between the Catholics and the Protestants would leave its mark from the moment the policy of Protestant Ascendancy was formed and, in many ways, the mark remains today.

It is often impossible to discuss the history of one country without also addressing the impact of events on a global scale, and this perhaps no more stark than in the history we have delved into in this book. While the conflict and struggle may have been born in

Ireland, it spread, and was changed and helped to evolve, by the involvement of other nations across the world.

It is clearly impossible, for instance, to address the history of many areas of America, without also understanding how what was happening over the Atlantic impacted that country. When the famine began to take root in Ireland and simply feeding one's family became a matter of survival, millions of people fled to a place they felt would hold a future for them.

This mass immigration had such a deep impact on America and Ireland that it became an almost surreal concept that the humble potato changed the face of two nations forever.

Immigration is never easy for anyone. Leaving everything you know behind and heading off into uncharted territory is frightening, and there are very few, if any, countries in the world whose people would wholly and unconditionally embrace what they might see as an invasion of unskilled and poverty-stricken people.

Although for the Irish the language was not an issue when arriving in America, almost everything else would have been a massive culture shock. Then, they found that, although they could eat in America, almost all the other issues they had in Ireland had followed them there—or rather, they'd been there all along, too.

As we have learned about the difficulties the people of Ireland have faced throughout history, it is not hard to understand how the generational trauma has impacted how many see the world. As opportunities and freedoms have leveled out, this will hopefully work its way out of the generations to come. However, for the Irish and Irish-American individuals we discussed in this book, the darkness of what their forefathers had experienced definitely shaped them.

As we have looked at the various facets of Irish history, including the many organizations that rose up, both for and against independence and reunification, it becomes clear how intrinsically-linked the growth of Irish organized crime has been to conflict, the desire for freedom, and the need to stand up against establishment.

Many early Irish-American organized crime groups used some of their profits to donate to the cause back home, and when that cause was, at least partially achieved, they simply continued on with the profit-making. By the same token, many more political groups, such as the IRA, are believed to have used organized crime methods to raise funds, and also set their organizations up in much the same way as gangs.

Often when Irish organized crime is discussed, the same individuals are brought forward as the main players throughout history. In this book, we've presented some lesser known individuals, as well as the gangs they started or belonged to, and a far more intricate picture is presented. Indeed, it seems that, at least in America, Irish influence on organized crime was profound, and if it hadn't been for a few instances of circumstance, the Irish may have been the prominent crime family, rather than the Italians.

For the most part, the idea that in the American mob underworld, the Italians work on their own and keep the profits to those of their own heritage is common. However, as we have seen, this is not entirely true. In fact, there have been instances of crossover and the various families and gangs working together to achieve a common goal of earning as much illicit profit as possible.

There is certainly an aspect of Irish-American organized crime that stands out and that is the violence with which it is often perpetrated. It would be unfair to class an entire people by the actions of their criminal element, but it is also not entirely possible to separate the traumatic history of the Irish from the way they would go on to carry out their crimes.

Indeed, the fact that many Irish crime groups are family-based, means generations of people have grown up around crime and violence, and this is always going to have a significant impact on future generations. If you have grown up exposed to ongoing death and violence, it becomes far easier to accept and perpetrate this yourself.

One can only wonder what the landscape of organized crime within both Ireland and America would look like today if that strain of potato blight had not crept into Ireland's crops.

The retelling and understanding of the history of Irish organized crime is not only important for curiosity's sake. In understanding how we came to be where we are today, in this respect, we can perhaps more deeply appreciate the complexities of all forms of crime. Crime, whether organized or not, is rarely only about money. It is often part of a rich history that begins to fully present itself when we dig and ask questions.

Today, we see drugs becoming the major commodity among organized crime groups. We see Irish mob members allying themselves with other international gangsters to form super cartels, and the future, at least for organized criminals, is seemingly bright.

Perhaps in two decades we will look back at this time as a period in which a new type of organized criminal was born. However, no matter how different Irish organized criminals look and behave in the future, there is no doubt that their past can never be completely separated from their present.

REFERENCES

Arthur, P. (n.d.). Sinn Féin - Policy and structure | Britannica. Www.britannica.com. https://www.britannica.com/topic/Sinn-Fein/Policy-and-structure

Arthur, P., & Cowell-Meyers, K. (2019). Irish Republican Army | History, Attacks, & Facts. In Encyclopædia Britannica. https://www.britannica.com/topic/Irish-Republican-Army

Arthur, P., & Cowell-Meyers, K. (n.d.). Ulster Volunteer Force | Northern Ireland military organization [1966]. Encyclopedia Britannica. https://www.britannica.com/topic/Ulster-Volunteer-Force-Northern-Ireland-1966

Bailey, B. (2017, May 21). Irish mob allegedly tries to silence witnesses in Oklahoma City shootout. Oklahoman.com. https://www.oklahoman.com/article/5549749/irish-mob-allegedly-tries-to-silence-witnesses-in-oklahoma-city-shootout

REFERENCES

Barry, M. B. (2020, June 3). The Irish War of Independence as seen by the international press. The Irish Times. https://www.irishtimes.com/culture/the-irish-war-of-independence-as-seen-by-the-international-press-1.4193775

Britannica. (n.d.). Ulster Defence Association | Irish paramilitary group. Encyclopedia Britannica. https://www.britannica.com/topic/Ulster-Defence-Association

Cunningham, J., & Lehr, D. (n.d.). Whitey Bulger | Biography, Crimes, & Facts. Encyclopedia Britannica. https://www.britannica.com/biography/Whitey-Bulger

Duggan, J. (2020, February 7). Brexit Has Revived the Prospect of a United Ireland. Could It Actually Happen? Time. https://time.com/5779707/irish-reunification-likelihood/

Forsyth, O. (2019, February 13). Irish Eddie Boyle - Gambino Associate. The Irish Mob. https://theirishmob.com/irish-eddie-boyle-gambino-associate/

Gannon, D. (n.d.). January 1919: the Irish Republic, the League of Nations and a new world order. The Conversation. https://theconversation.com/january-1919-the-irish-republic-the-league-of-nations-and-a-new-world-order-109524

Irish Central. (n.d.). TOP TEN IRISH GANGSTERS – Celtic Life International. Celtic Life. Retrieved February 22, 2022, from https://celticlifeintl.com/top-ten-irish-gangsters/

Jones, T. K. (1987, March 22). IRISH TROUBLES, AMERICAN MONEY. Washington Post. https://www.washingtonpost.com/archive/opinions/1987/03/22/irish-troubles-american-money/593e3941-826e-4719-bc79-8eb528f8ac70/

Library of Congress. (n.d.-b). Irish-Catholic Immigration to America | Irish | Immigration and Relocation in U.S. History | Classroom Materials at the Library of Congress | Library of Congress. Library of Congress, Washington, D.C. 20540 USA. https://www.loc.gov/classroom-materials/immigration/irish/irish-catholic-immigration-to-america/#:~:text=It%20is%20esti-mated%20that%20as

McDowell, J. (2021, January 6). Australian crime lord who ran counterfeiting op with PIRA dies aged 94. Sundayworld. https://www.sundayworld.com/crime/world-crime/flamboyant-oz-crime-lord-murray-stewart-riley-who-ran-counterfeiting-op-with-provos-dies-39934067.html

NORAID. (2019, September 22). Wikipedia. https://en.wikipedia.org/wiki/NORAID

O'Keeffe, C. (2021, September 14). Irish drug gangs linked to Italian mafia in EU cocaine boom. Irish Examiner. https://www.irishexaminer.com/news/arid-40697471.html

Petruzzello, M. (n.d.). Capuchin Franciscan order. Retrieved March 12, 2022, from https://www.britannica.com/topic/Capuchins

Roseingrave, L. (2021, April 18). Reindeer bone found in north Cork to alter understanding of Irish human history. Irish Examiner. https://www.irishexaminer.com/news/arid-40269116.html

Seamus Hanratty. (2019, July 26). The day the Irish Mob nearly wiped out the Italian Mafia in New York City. IrishCentral.com; IrishCentral. https://www.irishcentral.com/roots/history/irish-mob-italian-mafia-new-york

Stanyard, J., & Tagziria, L. (2020, March 4). Will Brexit see organized crime taking back control? Global Initiative. https://globalinitiative.net/analysis/organized-crime-brexit/

Watchmojo.com. (2011, June 2). The Irish Mafia and the History of Organized Crime. Www.youtube.com. https://www.youtube.com/watch?v=8UMxEeB6Ico

Wikipedia Contributors. (2019, February 8). The Troubles. Wikipedia; Wikimedia Foundation. https://en.wikipedia.org/wiki/The_Troubles

Wikipedia Contributors. (2019b, August 25). Westies. Wikipedia; Wikimedia Foundation. https://en.wikipedia.org/wiki/Westies

Wikipedia Contributor. (2022, February 20). Moroccan mafia. Wikipedia. https://en.wikipedia.org/wiki/Moroccan_mafia#Birth_of_international_drug_networks_(1995%E2%80%932006)

Wikipedia Contributor. (2022a, February 17). Kevin Weeks. Wikipedia. https://en.wikipedia.org/wiki/Kevin_Weeks

Wikipedia Contributors. (2022a, January 18). Stephen Flemmi. Wikipedia. https://en.wikipedia.org/wiki/Stephen_Flemmi

Wikipedia Contributors. (2022a, January 15). Johnny Martorano. Wikipedia. https://en.wikipedia.org/wiki/Johnny_Martorano

Wikipedia Contributor. (2022a, February 6). Roach Guards. Wikipedia. https://en.wikipedia.org/wiki/Roach_Guards

Wikipedia Contributor. (2021, December 12). Patrick Nee. Wikipedia. https://en.wikipedia.org/wiki/Patrick_Nee

Wikipedia Contributors. (2022d, February 21). Elmer "Trigger" Burke. Wikipedia; Wikimedia Foundation. https://en.wikipedia.org/wiki/Elmer_%22Trigger%22_Burke

Wikipedia Contributors. (2021, September 16). William Colbeck (gangster). Wikipedia. https://en.wikipedia.org/wiki/William_Colbeck_(gangster)

Wikipedia Contributors. (2022a, January 1). Mad Dog Coll. Wikipedia. https://en.wikipedia.org/wiki/Mad_Dog_Coll

ABOUT THE AUTHOR

David Carlton is a child of 1970's and 80's Britain. Growing up in a period of terrorist threats and atrocities developed his keen interest in modern history and investigations into the "why" of global events behind the "what".

David is married, with three children and lives in Bedfordshire, England.